we are

ONE!

lance

Other Books by Lance Secretan

Inspire! What Great Leaders Do
Spirit@Work®: Bringing Spirit and Values to Work
Inspirational Leadership®: Destiny, Calling and Cause
Reclaiming Higher Ground: Creating Organizations
  That Inspire the Soul
Living the Moment: A Sacred Journey
The Way of the Tiger: Gentle Wisdom for Turbulent Times
The Masterclass: Modern Fables for Working and Living
Managerial Moxie: The 8 Proven Steps to Empowering
  Employees and Supercharging Your Company

CDs by Lance Secretan

Inspire! What Great Leaders Do
Inspirational Leadership®: Destiny, Calling and Cause
Reclaiming Higher Ground: Creating Organizations
  That Inspire the Soul
Living the Moment: A Sacred Journey
The Keys to the CASTLE: The Magic of Higher
  Ground Leadership®
The New Story of Leadership: Reclaiming Higher Ground
Values-centered Leadership®: A Model for Work and Life
The Calling Meditation

Videos and DVDs by Lance Secretan

Inspire! What Great Leaders Do
Inspirational Leadership®: Destiny, Calling and Cause
Reclaiming Higher Ground: Creating Organizations
  That Inspire the Soul
The Keys to the CASTLE: The Magic of Higher
  Ground Leadership®
Values-centered Leadership®: A Model for Work and Life

ONE

The Art and Practice of Conscious Leadership

Lance H. K. Secretan

THE SECRETAN CENTER INC.

Published by The Secretan Center Inc.
Caledon, Ontario, Canada

Library and Archives Canada Cataloguing in Publication

Secretan, Lance H. K.
    One : the art and practice of conscious leadership / Lance Secretan.

Includes index.

ISBN 0-9733115-5-X

1. Leadership.   2. Conduct of life.   3. Self-realization.   I. Title.

BF637.L4S42 2006   158'.4   C2005-907646-1

In the spirit of oneness, no trees were cut to manufacture this book—it has been printed on 100% post-consumer waste recycled paper.

Cover design: John Lee, Heidy Lawrance Associates
Text design: Heidy Lawrance, www.hlacreative.com

Printed in Canada

We are part of the whole which we call the universe,
but it is an optical delusion of our mind
that we think we are separate.
This separateness is like a prison for us.
Our job is to widen the circle of compassion
so we feel connected to all people
and all situations.

Albert Einstein

TABLE OF CONTENTS

ACKNOWLEDGMENTS

THIS BOOK IS the result of the input of many loving souls.

I have spent much time with the remarkable people whose stories are told in this book, including Bernie Bredschneider, Rinaldo Brutoco, Don Campbell, Sue Ellen Cooper, Kirk Hoessle, Dave Loney, Dave Mowat, Amelie Noiseux, Paula Rosario, Adele Azar-Rucquoi and Jim Rucquoi, Scott Simmie, Frank Stronach, and George Zimmer. Without exception, they are exemplary leaders. I thank them all for their time and commitment, in some cases courage, and in all cases, generous cooperation.

My colleague Sarah Grimmer has modeled the CASTLE Principles every day in our work together. Generously sharing her wise and insightful counsel, she has made an enormous contribution to this book.

Ken Jacobsen reviewed numerous drafts and offered impeccable wisdom and excellent suggestions, many of which were woven into this book, improving it greatly.

My longtime friend and editor, Simone Gabbay, is a wonderful writer, editor, and, most important, creative partner. Her gentle, astute, and imaginative ideas have become part of the tapestry of *ONE*.

An international community grew around this book as it was being conceived, written, and developed. This became a remarkable team of advisors, co-creators, technical specialists, marketers, missionaries, consultants, reviewers, friends, and a deep and valuable resource to whom I frequently turned and on whom I relied. I am immensely grateful to John Halstead, Anna Harper, Elizabeth Jetton, Rob Katz, Laurie Kennedy, Shonnie Lavender, Sue Lindsay, Susan Nind, Anne Preston, Rob Ryder, and Charleen Tupper. A larger circle of several hundred individuals from around the world generously helped us with advice, ideas, research, and loving criticism—modeling beautifully the principles of this book. Our many international conference calls, e-mails, conversations, and visits added greater richness and clarity to *ONE*.

Tracey Gilmore, Tricia Field, and Rae Brown have been a constantly supportive team at the Secretan Center, and their diverse gifts have made all the difference for me in ways that I deeply appreciate.

Thanks to Boshira Toomey for his insightful explanations of the work of Donald Winnicott, to Ron Szymanski for his helpful input, and to Don Bastian for his valuable editing and creative ideas regarding the structure of the book. Converting the words into physical form was brilliantly undertaken by the design team at Heidy Lawrance Associates and Fred Cheetham and the printing team at Friesens, a 100-year-old Mennonite-owned firm that is a living model of the CASTLE Principles.

Spirit, the wonder dog, kept me company during many long hours of writing and contributed her companionship, canine counsel, and limitless unconditional love.

And—of course the last shall be first—my amazing wife, Tricia, as always, has been my rock, toughest critic, and greatest supporter. I shall love her forever. We are one.

PREFACE

IN 1980, I RESIGNED as chief executive of a large multinational company and joined the university, where I eagerly embarked on a new adventure: transforming myself from practicing CEO to teacher of current and future CEOs. During the summer of that year, I prepared for my new duties by studying 150 books about leadership, strategy, and what it takes to run successful organizations. I was eager to learn what the leading thinkers and scholars on this subject had to say. But the experience left me with a strange feeling, for very few of these books described what I had actually experienced as a leader during the previous 14 years.

Unable to find a textbook that addressed the subject as I had experienced it, I wrote my own. It was called *Managerial Moxie* and chronicled the journey of my team in resurrecting a moribund business called Manpower Limited and turning it into a world-class, internationally renowned organization. At 496 pages, filled with complex diagrams, charts, matrixes, models, formulae, and theories, it weighed in at 1.4 pounds.

Managerial Moxie conformed to the writing formula required by the culture of the university. This formula demanded deep research, empirical validation of theories, double-blind studies, and peer-referenced material that, after being reviewed and endorsed by various committees, would become part of the curriculum. I realized that this had caused me to write an unnecessarily complicated book about a subject that is really quite simple. Our academic institutions sometimes create an artifice of complexity and separateness that is not reflective of reality.

Since then, I have written 14 books in which I have attempted to unfold various theories that identify the characteristics of conscious leadership and living an inspiring life. What I have observed is that leadership emanates not from an external thing, but from our own heart, mind, and soul. This process causes others to be inspired, and when they are, causes them to inspire still others, who, in turn, inspire all those with whom they connect. All of this eventually vibrates into an inspired world—oneness in action.

A body of work has been developed during the hundreds of retreats, coaching sessions, workshops, and consulting assignments that have been conducted around the world based on the ideas expressed in the following pages. Called *Higher Ground Leadership*®, it has been reworked, refined, and polished by many over the years, becoming the metatheory it is today. Although the six underpinning concepts of Higher Ground Leadership, called the CASTLE Principles (Courage, Authenticity, Service, Truthfulness, Love, and Effectiveness), have been taught to, and practiced by, thousands of people, they have never been laid out succinctly in book form—until now. *ONE*, which you are holding in your hands, is the result.

As I have spent more time in the world, I've come to realize that living an inspiring life and making the world a better place are not complex subjects. As a matter of fact, they are very simple and may be summarized this way: *We are one, and the world would be a better place if we loved each other and told the truth.* This can be taken as a deep metaphysical statement (which I invite you to consider, although that is not my primary intent) or as a pragmatic description of reality.

So, this book is a much smaller book than my previous ones. If I felt there were a market for such a thing, I would perhaps write a one-page book that would simply say, "If we understand that we are one and love each other and tell the truth, we will each become more inspired and fulfilled, and the world will be a better place." However, there is not yet a tradition for one-page books! The first-century Babylonian Jewish sage Hillel wrote, "What is hateful to you, do not do to another. This is the whole of the Law, the rest is commentary. Go, learn the commentary." Every great teacher in history has said something similar: *We are one; love each other and tell the truth.* But we must keep saying it again and in the language of each new generation.

Blaise Pascal once said, "I have made this letter longer than usual, because I lack the time to make it short." There has been enough time to keep this book simple and brief. In addition to reintroducing the concepts of being one, loving each other, and telling the truth, I will propose four more essential characteristics of the inspiring life—six in total—but it really is as simple as that!

I do not for a minute wish to suggest that it is easy to love each other and tell the truth—far from it. But it is simple. And when we love each other and tell the truth, we are one. Understanding this, and learning how to live it, is the heart of this book's message.

Carl Jung wrote the following words in the final paragraph of a letter to one of his colleagues: "You get nowhere with theories. Try to be simple and always take the next step... So climb down from the mountain...and follow your nose. This is your way and the straightest." That is how I have attempted to develop the

CASTLE Principles and write this book. I hope that *ONE* will be another guide on your path to oneness in your life and deepen your practice as a conscious leader.

INTRODUCTION

THIS BOOK DESCRIBES how we have come to think in compartmentalized, atomized ways (which I will call *atomism* or *separateness*), and how we can once again think holistically (which I will call *holism* or *oneness*), and therefore find real meaning in leadership and in life.

The *New Oxford Dictionary of English* defines holism as—

> *The theory that parts of the whole are in intimate connection, such that they cannot exist independently of the whole, or cannot be understood without reference to the whole, which is thus regarded as greater than the sum of its parts.*

It defines its opposite, atomism, as—

> *A theoretical approach that regards something as interpretable through analysis into distinct, separable, and independent elementary components.*

In Part One of this book, ***The Art of Oneness***, we explore the emergence of a renewed and powerful desire for oneness in our generation. I will show how advances in technology and communications are a major impetus of this desire, and that the desire goes even deeper: it is a longing to regain the myth, mystery, and magic of a oneness we experienced before the dawn of separateness created by the ideas introduced in philosophy and science. This appreciation of our oneness is what each of us is yearning to find in our leaders, and by which, deep inside, each of us aspires to be guided as we lead.

Part Two, *The Practice of Oneness*, explores how we can reclaim our innate sense of oneness by delving deeply into, and living, each of the CASTLE Principles: Courage, Authenticity, Service, Truthfulness, Love, and Effectiveness, thus enabling us to see the sacred connections between everyone and everything—the oneness of people and things.

Every great manifesto, like a pearl in an oyster, is a beautiful article that was initiated by an irritation. The U.S. Declaration of Independence, Britain's Magna Carta, Czechoslovakia's Charter 77, and the Canadian Charter of Rights and Freedoms all came about in response to the increasing pain of separation and a corresponding yearning for oneness. They are descriptions of the problems encountered, written in reverse, often in prose that inspires. This process of retracing our steps to a higher ideal is also how the CASTLE Principles were birthed.

Like all fundamental concepts, these are simple ideas that are well known to most of us. The new part is shifting from talking about them to doing them—to deeply living these principles ourselves, rather than telling others to do so. For when *fully lived*, these life-attitudes are profoundly transformative and inspiring to ourselves and others.

There is nothing new to learn here, no great theory, breakthrough, or equation, because these are concepts that are within us already. At some stage in our lives, they were fully lived, typically earlier in our life journey. Now, however, they may have become lost, and we yearn to reclaim them. Consider the CASTLE principle of *Courage*, for example. When we had fewer stakes in the game of life—no mortgage or car payments, no executive position to hold on to—we were naturally more courageous. Speaking our truth, and acting in accordance with it, was easy. As the years passed and we accumulated possessions and responsibilities, we inversely became more cynical, frightened, and drained of the power and passion from which our courage was drawn.

The aim of this book, therefore, is *to inspire you to recall when you were at your personal best and to live at this peak again.* Through living the CASTLE Principles, we will inspire each other and see the world not as separate, unconnected parts, but as one.

I did not discover these concepts. They discovered me. I asked people what they felt were the characteristics of ineffective relationships, whether at home or at work, in politics, religion, academia, or our marriages, or among our families and friends. My research showed that people were typically turned off by others who were not courageous, authentic, serving, truthful, loving, and effective. It made no difference whether they were CEOs, stay-at-home moms, or athletes—or whether they came from different countries and cultures. In fact, my colleagues and I have found that there is very little difference in what constitutes meaning and fulfillment at work for people, regardless of their demographic or cultural origins. This is corroborated in a 2005 survey by Sirota Survey Intelligence based in Purchase, New York, which reports: "More than half of human resource professionals surveyed erroneously believe there are major differences between what people of different generations, cultures, and countries expect from their jobs. There are three basic goals that the vast majority of employees want from their work, regardless of their ages, cultures, or geographies." These are:

- Achievement, or pride in one's work—being *one* with what we do;
- Camaraderie, or positive and productive relationships with one's co-workers—being *one* with others; and,
- Equity, or being treated fairly in matters such as pay, benefits, and job security—making the work effort *one* with the reward received.

This data is based on surveys of about 3.5 million employees at hundreds of organizations in all sectors. Jeffrey Saltzman, chief executive officer of Sirota, says, "While a kernel of truth may exist to some manager beliefs about generational and cultural differences outside of the work environment, managers who are guided by these differences within the working environment are, in fact, operating under a myth. For example, if managers expect people from Generation X to be very different, then they may create policies based on their expectations, rather than the reality of what people want from work. Not only is this a waste of time and resources, it can become a self-fulfilling prophecy—a vicious circle."

The reality is that we are one, and our attempts to separate people by classifying them and "slicing and dicing" data about them can lead us to obsolete separateness-thinking, which is counterproductive.

Thus, it was a short intellectual leap towards the observation that living the opposite of the limiting deficiencies—lack of courage, inauthenticity, failure to serve, truthlessness, lovelessness, and ineffectiveness—would reveal the proficiencies that would make all the difference. This is how the CASTLE Principles were born.

In explaining these principles, I am proposing that we reframe our view of leadership—not just in the context of work, but in the larger context of life. Why do I use this formulation, rather than the more usual distinction between "work and life"? Because "work and life" is a limiting, fragmenting mindset based on separateness. It assumes a separation of work and life, and of course, there are not two things to separate—there is only *one* thing—it's called *life*, of which work is just a part. The endless search to balance these two is thus a hopeless one, because modern communications, the global nature of the workplace, the changing nature of what we call "work," and the adaptations of culture accentuate the obvious: that "balance" is irrelevant. Such attitudes emphasize our tendency to practice separateness thinking. Life can be perceived as one again when we seek to be inspiring, conscious leaders living fully integrated lives. And we are all leaders from our first breath—who can ignore the demands of an insistent baby? The challenge, then, is not how we can balance work and life, but how we can lead *integrated* lives through the realization that all the parts are really one.

This book was written for leaders in every aspect of life's spectrum—managers, consultants, executives, CEOs, organizational-development and human-resource professionals, workshop and seminar leaders, supervisors, parents, teachers, coaches, mentors, clergy, public servants, not-for-profit professionals, therapists—in fact, all of us who are dedicated to serving, leading, and guiding others—helping them, as well as ourselves, to achieve greater worth and meaning in life.

I have included many luminous stories about people and organizations that have successfully learned how to appreciate the oneness of life and are doing so by living the CASTLE Principles. In many ways, this is a "how to" book, but it might be just as helpful to describe it as a collection of the stories of remarkable people practicing ideas and theories that truly work.

PART ONE

The Art of Oneness

1

THE NEW IMPERATIVE OF ONENESS

W E HAVE BEEN LIVING with an illusion: that we are separate. Whenever we experience pain or sadness, it is because we have become separated from what, or whom, we love. And whenever we are inspired or joyful, it is because we are one with what, or whom, we love. All human challenges and successes can be explained through this awareness.

> If we have no peace, it is because we have forgotten we belong to each other.
>
> *Mother Teresa*

When we are in love with someone, it is as if we are one: two souls, one flame. That is because we are.

When we love doing something, or something makes our hearts soar, we feel as if we are one with it, because we are.

When we ache over the imperiled state of nature or the rising level of violence in the world, we ache because we feel the same pain. We share it because we are one.

Imagine a bright, sunny day. You are relaxing at your favorite sidewalk bistro. The enticing shrimp cocktail you ordered arrives, and you marvel at its beauty and presentation. As you relish the gift of brilliance from your chef, your mind wanders. You ask yourself the question that often crosses your mind when you encounter creativity, excellence, or mastery: "How do they do that?" In this case, you wonder, "Where did this food come from? What did it take to prepare it so beautifully? Who was involved in making this special treat?" In your reverie, you are transported far away, to seafaring nations and peoples. More than a billion people reside within 100 miles of the ocean, from which many of them derive their livelihoods, while all depend on a measure of stability between sea and land.

World shrimp production has ballooned from 2.9 million metric tons to 4.5 million in the past 15 years alone, with Asian production leading the world. Thailand, now the largest producer, earns $2 billion annually from its shrimping industry. America imports 88 percent of its $4-billion shrimp purchases, and prices have dropped by 50 percent in the past ten years. Half of the shrimp production is farmed. Fishing nations have mastered shrimp farming so well that it now accounts for 50 percent of world production. The shrimp offered in restaurants and food stores today costs only a dollar a pound to produce.

But to create shrimp farms, it is necessary to remove mangroves. Mangroves once covered more than three-quarters of the world's tropical coastline. Today, they cover less than 37 percent. Just 50 years ago, the shores along the rim of the Indian Ocean were ringed with endless acres of mangroves—swampy rainforests hugging the edges of both land and sea. Mangroves are storehouses of biodiversity, home to the world's richest variety of salt-tolerant trees, ferns, and shrubs. Hundreds of different birds live in the mangroves, which also shelter migratory species. Mangroves are rich in sea life, including plankton, mollusks, and shell- and fin-fish. They are well-populated with crocodiles, monkeys, wild cats, lizards, and sea turtles.

As the region's developing countries have expanded and diversified their economies, protective reefs, sand dunes, and mangroves along coastlines have been steadily removed. In the past few decades, more than 30 percent of the world's mangrove forests, covering tens of thousands of miles of coastline, have been destroyed to make room for shrimp farms. Shrimp farming has resulted in beaches being cleared of mangroves and in an enormous rise of tourism, hotels, big cities, and other coastal developments.

On their way to their fishing boats early on the morning of December 26, 2004, fishermen noticed an odd absence of the usual wildlife found along their paths, but paid little attention to it. As they began trawling, there seemed to be an extraordinary abundance of fish: mackerel, squid, red snapper, sardines, and white snapper. They had never seen such profusion or diversity. In fact, yellow catfish, tiger fish, and other species not usually seen in these waters were, for the first time, remarkably abundant.

On that morning, fishermen long used to variable fishing conditions were giddy with excitement, hauling in their catch as fast as they could, convinced that their singular luck could not last for long.

During the previous three weeks, there had been a strange and total absence of fish, and the ocean had become unusually deep. And at this moment, very strangely, the tide seemed to be receding further and faster than they had ever seen before. Coral reefs appeared in only four meters of water where the sea was normally 20 meters deep. Something odd was happening. The tide was supposed to be coming in, but it was going out. Nobody on the beach was paying attention, but a kilometer of sand had replaced the space where normally there was sea. Fishing boats were sitting on wet sand.

In the distance, perhaps a kilometer away, a large wave could be seen—angular, black, and moving very, very fast. After the tsunami hit, 300,000 people died. In the ensuing chaos and destruction, one million jobs were lost in Indonesia and Sri Lanka alone.

Fewer casualties were experienced where mangrove forests remained, for example in Pichavaram and Muthupet in South India. Close to the epicenter of the tsunami, on Nias Island,

Indonesia, people were protected by mangroves. Burma and the Maldives suffered less damage because their mangroves and coral reefs remained largely intact.

Sitting in the bistro, you might think that a shrimp cocktail, world shrimp prices, friends on vacation, unemployment, the silence of animals, mangroves, tsunamis, and death and destruction in twelve different countries were all separate events. But we are part of one universal web. All these parts are intimately, exquisitely, and invisibly connected—they are one.

What I have described above is far from being a complete review of all the possible impacts and outcomes of nations hungry for shrimp, and we may never even know or make the connections necessary to identify them all. But we can become more aware of the notion of oneness and live our lives in a way that recognizes the sacred connections between everything and considers the implications of all our actions on the whole.

When we lead from this place in our hearts, it shows.

Making Oneness Practical

America West flight attendants' union vice-president Bill Lehman credits CEO Doug Parker for the survival of the airline during an extraordinarily difficult time for the industry. "Had Doug not been in power in September 2001, we wouldn't be here today," said Lehman, who has been with America West for 16 years.

Parker serves meals to workers at Thanksgiving and Christmas and works on the ramp as a baggage handler. "You just don't see that," Lehman said. "It is really pretty impressive." America West pilots' union chairman, J. R. Baker, is equally impressed. Parker took time out from a Phoenix golf tournament to intervene in a case involving Baker's son, who has lymphoma, by personally persuading the insurance company to allow Baker's son back in the hospital after a relapse. "He is a good guy," Baker said of Parker.

Parker sees himself as one with—not separate from—his colleagues at all levels. And when he negotiates with unions, he is treated the same way—as one—which is why the company goes from strength to strength. Its customers, vendors, employees, communities, and regulators are all one. In 2005, America West merged with US Airways to become the world's largest low-fare airline.

Wherever we are, whatever we do, think, or feel, we are connected through sacred pathways to each other and to all that is—the reality of oneness. When we grow our awareness of this reality, we grow our capacity for conscious leadership.

Turning Away from Separateness

According to the Conference Board, 40 percent of employees feel disconnected from their companies, and two out of three do not identify or feel motivated to support their employer's business objectives. Some 25 percent are "just showing up to collect a paycheck." In one mid-western university, a study showed that between 1988 and 2001, there was a dramatic increase in mental health problems reported by students. The numbers seeking help for depression doubled, and the number contemplating suicide tripled. The National Institute of Mental Health predicts that 13 percent of Americans (19 million) between the ages of 18 and 54 suffer from anxiety disorders and 9.5 percent from depressive disorders. The World Health Organization forecasts that by 2020, the share of "global disease burden" (the number of years of life lost to premature death or disability) will rise from 10.5 percent to 15 percent. The sadness and unhappiness of separation come with a heavy price.

In the past few years, we have become increasingly aware that separateness not only defies reality, it also brings about a sickness of the body—and worse, of the soul. Along with this, we have also become aware that the world is smaller, more interdependent, and integrated. As we will see, the desire for, and experience of, oneness is not new. However, there is today a new awareness being felt and heard across the world that calls us all to return to oneness. Community is growing in importance, and privacy has become history. The new reality—novel for some, and everyday experience for others—is that we are one.

We are connected in ways we did not see before. Anheuser-Busch, which uses Missouri-grown rice to make beer, became anxious when it heard about the plans of Ventria Biosciences to plant fields in Missouri with transgenic rice containing human genes. The additional genes cause the plant to produce two proteins which Ventria intends to use to treat stomach disorders. Anheuser-Busch realized that the transgenic plants and seeds could migrate to the food crops and, eventually, might modify their beer. When the company announced that it would boycott Missouri rice if Ventria proceeded, the biotech company decided to plant the rice elsewhere. Everything in our lives is connected. We are one.

- If we bulldoze suppliers to provide more services and higher quality at lower prices and, by doing so, eventually drive them out of business, we will both lose, because suppliers and customers are one.
- If we have a rancorous exchange with our spouse, it isn't just the other party who is hurt. We are both hurt because our relationship—our oneness—is strained. This damages our partnership and therefore both of us, along with our children and friends, our work, and our health and well-being.[1]
- If I throw my soda can out of my car window while driving, I may think that the litter I have thrown on the road is no longer

---

1. A study published in the December 2005 issue of *Archives of General Psychiatry* suggests that spouses engaged in hostile relationships have consistently elevated stress levels that significantly impede their bodies' wound-healing capacity and raise blood levels of pro-inflammatory cytokines, which have been linked to a higher risk of developing depression, heart disease, osteoporosis, arthritis, type 2 diabetes, cancer, and general physical decline.

part of my world after I have moved on, but I would be wrong. If millions of others do the same, rivers will become polluted and my drinking water will be at risk. The Earth is not an open system—it is a closed system.

- If I cheat or steal from my employees, customers, or suppliers, I may think that I can get away with it, but this is a misconception, as we have learned from the malfeasance and downfall of too many corporate leaders.

- When we inspire a child to do something extraordinary, we change the world, because we are one.

In these, and many other examples cited in this book, there are always causes and effects. (These are the terms we use in the West, but the process is known as *karma* in the East.) There are never actions without consequences—anywhere—because we are one.

The depth of our self-deception, caused by our belief in, and commitment to, separateness—isolating and disconnecting aspects of our lives—has become breathtaking. Consider what happened when Bernie Ebbers, the disgraced, then 63-year-old former CEO of WorldCom, was sentenced to 25 years in jail for orchestrating an $11-billion accounting fraud, the biggest in the nation's history. His lawyers asked for leniency on the basis of their client's largesse and support of charitable causes! This suggests a bizarre mind-trick that stealing with one hand and supporting charities with the other represent separate activities, even when carried out by the same person! We continue in this illusion when we hurt others while believing that we are not hurting ourselves. The truth is quite otherwise. When we hurt a customer, we hurt ourselves, because the customer becomes an ex-customer—and because we share the same world.

The illusion is that we are separate: that the gum someone stuck under their seat in the movie theater would become part of another's world after they left; that my anger, when transferred to you, becomes your problem, not mine; that my department—or even company—is separate from yours; that if I crush a competitor, it affects them, but not me. The illusion is that we are separate from one another, separate from our actions, separate from other regions, cultures, religions, companies, and beliefs. When we act as if we were separate—for example, when we deliver shoddy service to customers, or exploit employees—that act of separateness creates a bigger wave of separateness.

People are feeling increasingly separate from business today, and this is counterproductive for the corporate world. In almost every field, we are being subjected to the powerful awakening that there is no separateness, only oneness. Martin Luther King Jr. said, "Injustice anywhere is a threat to justice everywhere."

The air that I breathe is essential for my existence—to exist, I must breathe. Therefore, I am one with the air, for when the air ceases, so do I. In the same way, the water and I are also one. And the water *and* the air—*and you and I*—are all one, for we all exist interdependently. Therefore, we, and everything around us, are one.

The wave is not separate from the ocean; the oxygen in water is not separate from the hydrogen; the wave is not separate from the particle; I am not separate from you. In fact, nothing is separate from anything. We are one.

Transparency Reveals Our Oneness

Corporations, governments, health care, education, law enforcement, charities, associations, and religious groups are under more intense scrutiny than ever before, operating with the growing awareness that they will be held accountable for their actions—that everything they do may, sooner or later, become subject to investigation, audit, and media surveillance. Privacy is history. The Sarbanes-Oxley Act of the United States and the new European international capital standard, known as Basle II, are just two of many new initiatives that are changing the game, requiring stringent new levels of openness and fair practice in corporate governance. Although Sarbanes-Oxley is American law, it applies to any organization from any country doing business in the United States.

On a trip to England, I was surprised to see a headline declaring, "Elliott Spitzer shakes up UK Insurance Industry"—this in reference to the probe into insurance industry practices by New York State's Attorney General in his home state. Note that we are referring here to *one* elected government attorney from *one* U.S. state who has impacted the lives and businesses of thousands of people all over the world. This one man has effected lower mutual fund fees, changed the structure of Wall Street research, forced drug companies to open up their clinical trials to public scrutiny, and overhauled the relationship between insurance companies and brokers—worldwide.

Technology Makes Us One

Technology is just one of many forces teaching us the reality that we are all connected, guiding us, sometimes reluctantly, into the glare of transparency and fairness. We are interconnected and interdependent in ways that seem more obvious than ever before. And technology is accentuating the transparency by helping to reveal *and* empower these connections as never before. We are one.[2]

In 1992, when underdog Korean presidential candidate Roh Moo Hyun's running mate, Chung Mong Joon, leader of the National Alliance 21 party, withdrew his support for Roh just seven hours before polls closed, things looked very bleak for the latter. Adding to his woes were the three leading newspapers, *Chosun Ilbo,*

---

2. Service-Oriented Architecture (SOA) is an example of the growing oneness in software, which, even when they are written in different languages and have different purposes, can work together for a common goal.

Joong-ang Ilbo, and *Dong-A Ilbo*, which were dismissing Roh as a dangerous leftist and declaring that he would be defeated. Early exit polls showed Roh trailing his opponent, Grand National Party leader Lee Hoi Chang, by a substantial margin.

Self-educated, Roh came from a poor family and in earlier years had been jailed for helping dissidents fight the military regimes of the past. In 1981, Roh defended a student who was arrested on trumped-up charges of anti-state activities, and much of his subsequent work had been as a human rights lawyer defending pro-democracy and labor-rights activists. This endeared him to students and young voters. Admiring his courage, integrity, and reputation as an independent outsider, they formed an Internet fan club to promote his future. In time, this band of supporters grew to 70,000 members and helped launch what has been called the Roh typhoon. The Internet enabled Roh to liberate himself from "black money"—corporate donations that are South Korea's traditional form of campaign financing. Largely through Internet-based campaign groups, Roh raised the equivalent of about $1 billion from more than 180,000 individual donors.

> I am only one, but still I am one. I cannot do everything, but still I can do something. I will not refuse to do the something I can do.
>
> *Helen Keller*

Thus it was that news of Roh's impending electoral defeat quickly circulated among young voters via Internet bulletin boards and cell phones operated by digitally savvy student supporters. One Internet site recorded three million hits from around midnight to about 3 a.m. on Election Day—some five to six times the average. Hundreds of thousands of Roh's young supporters made millions of cell phone calls, and 800,000 text messages flashed to the cell phones of their friends, urging them to go to the polls and vote for Roh.

By 2 p.m., another exit poll showed that Roh was leading Lee by 2 to 3 percent, and shortly after the polls closed, Roh was declared the winner.

Technology has become a remarkable gift, beyond others that we take so much for granted. It is a tool that, for the first time in history, has the power to wire the souls of the universe together—for good. The funeral of Princess Diana marked the first time in history when one story was shared with one billion people around the world simultaneously—on CNN.

Technology has raised the level of consciousness in the world by helping us to see how much we have in common, and causing us to understand that we are connected as one. Technology also offers the means to examine, endorse, or challenge the thoughts and actions of anyone on earth. A new age of relationships will flow from this—among members of society and between societies—based on the realization that we are all connected, that we are all part of one universal system.

Corporate leaders, government officials, church leaders, athletes, entertainers, even moms and dads, all are available for scrutiny. We have lost our separate, untouchable status. We have come to realize that we are all one and more similar to, than different from, one another. We are human, vulnerable, susceptible, brilliant, curious, and magnificent. We are capable of greatness and of making mistakes. We have learned that our idols who were portrayed in books and movies as charismatic leader prototypes are not, after all, immune to questioning, as issues pertaining to their business and personal ethics are openly discussed and disseminated more quickly and widely than ever before in the electronic, digital, and printed media. Not a single digit, or document, with our name on it is exempt from examination.

Since being formed in 2001, the phenomenal, self-organizing, Web-based free encyclopedia, Wikipedia, has become much larger than all existing encyclopedias, most of which were assembled and developed over far longer periods. It is a portent of how the Web attracts and embraces oneness—over half a million contributors offer articles and self-regulate the system, acting as one, and the average time it takes to detect, remove, or repair deliberate attempts to sabotage Wikipedia's trust and integrity is 1.7 seconds!

Whatever we create, we create not just for our (imagined) separate selves, but for us all, because, of course, we are one, and technology helps to smooth the path to oneness.

The Emergence of the Conscious Leader

Why is there an emerging interest in conscious leadership? One of the reasons is that our expectations of leaders and leadership are changing as we become more aware of the shortcomings of separateness thinking and the imperative of oneness.

In the past, we have made organizational leaders our icons. We have separated them from us by putting them on pedestals, worshiping their personalities, and singing their praises as if they were heroic saviors. Countless leadership theories have passed like meteorites in the night sky of history, and now we are reassessing many of them, along with our opinions of corporate leaders, some of whom made their fame and were exalted for practices like firing the lowest-performing 10 percent of their sales teams each year. We yearn for something more than this—something more honoring of our oneness.

The people we fire are also our customers, our friends, and members of our communities. To celebrate a company that "succeeds" by firing people might seem okay to some when it is happening in other companies, but it feels different when it is your company doing the firing, and you are the one being fired. Companies that "succeed" by one set of measures, but fail by another, or "succeed" at the expense of another, are practicing an obsolete concept: separateness. Today, consumers want to wear sneakers that are stylish and inexpensive, *and* they want the employees who make them to be fairly compensated for their work. These are signals that a new maturity is emerging, based on greater consciousness. We are realizing that we should help and support those who are confused, disadvantaged, or underperforming, instead of yelling at them or firing them—or demanding, rather than inspiring, higher performance. This represents a priceless strategic opportunity for those who are conscious, and a wake-up call for those who are not.

Countless organizations from Nike to McDonald's to Starbucks have transformed their policies in response to this new awareness. Starbucks, for example, through its supply chain member, Mississippi River Corporation, received first-ever approval from the Food and Drug Administration to incorporate 10 percent postconsumer fiber into its hot-beverage paper cups. The new cups reduce the company's use of tree fiber by more than five million pounds annually.

That is not to say that this shift in consciousness is going to be perfectly smooth or lead to immediate and successful transformation. We've been drawing our models of leadership from history, casting leadership in terms of heroes and miracle workers. In doing so, we have created a "cult of the personality." This can be seen everywhere, in the world of business, in sports, in entertainment. The relationship we have with those magnified personalities is based on dependency, power, and separateness. We have created our modern form of serfs and peasants. We should remind ourselves that history is full of examples of people who "buckled under" these types of leaders. Think of Genghis Khan, Mussolini, or Hitler, or any despotic, pathological leader. The human condition is malleable and vulnerable to the urgings of a Pol Pot, an Idi Amin, a Mao Tse-tung, or a Stalin. The direction humans take can easily be swayed by potent leaders if the relationship with their followers is rooted in separateness—the mistaken belief that the consequences of my actions are separate from me and are not now, and will not become, my problem. Like all radical changes, the move away from this thinking to models of conscious leadership based on oneness will be challenging.

In her research, Bernice Kanner, author of *Are You Normal About Money?* (Bloomberg Press, 2001), found that for $10 million,

25 percent of those surveyed would abandon all their friends and church or become a prostitute for a week, or change their race or sex. And 7 percent (this seems so incredible—one out of every 14 of us) would commit murder for this amount. But the margins between corruption and virtue are narrow. Most people surveyed said they would do these things for as little as $3 million, but definitely not for $2 million. Go figure! In our rational, material times, it seems we have our principles—attached to a certain price. This may also suggest something else, however: that although we inherently understand the principle of oneness, at the mundane levels we are prepared to act separately, until the going gets dangerous, when we instinctively resort to oneness again, because deep in our hearts, we *know* we need one another.

Throughout history, there have been numerous opportunities for leaders, through their personality and their demagoguery, to create armies of followers who would do all kinds of reprehensible things at their urging. This has been the dynamic of the ego-driven leadership style during the past thousand years. But it worked better (if "better" is an appropriate word here) in an era before our networks were democratized.

We are learning that the fear-based, egocentric leadership model—the leader as hero or charismatic personality—is ineffective. The results it produces are not consistent. As our societies move from a worldview based on separateness to one based on oneness, achieving results by fear-based measures is bound to be temporary. Parents who bribe and punish their children to achieve results; spouses who withhold emotional gifts from each other to control their relationship; politicians who make promises to secure votes; priests who guarantee salvation in exchange for doctrinal adherence; or companies that over-promise to make a sale—all rely on fear-based manipulations that will prove to be transitory and uninspiring because they are rooted in the illusion of separateness. They are trying to control and win, instead of connecting and cooperating, which creates oneness.

Today, we are tired of the "rational" ten-point plan for leadership that purports to provide a guaranteed outcome. Our ways of thinking in the post-9/11 era are very different. We are engaging leaders and programs in a much higher level of questioning. Today, we're looking at each other and asking, "Who are you really? What do you stand for and what values do you represent? What are the deeper and wider implications of your behavior? In what way have my actions contributed to your behavior? Are you more connected to the whole than to your ego?" We are looking for conscious leaders and teachers who are not merely doing what they can get away with, but who are loving and respectful of others and have a deep commitment to values and to living an inspiring life that is sensitive to everything and everyone. We're asking questions that attempt to move us towards a deeper sense of oneness.

And the inspiring bonus that flows to us all from this new thinking is the growing awareness of the good in people and their potential to contribute to greater oneness.

2

ONENESS LOST

ONENESS MAY BE the ideal, but separateness is the habit. And habits are hard to break.

For thousands of years, we have been perfecting our skills of separateness, hardwiring our thought processes, reasoning skills, education, media, relationships, politics, religions, organizations, and parenting practices. The world has become a patchwork of separateness. In all these fields, there are "right and wrong" and "good and bad" ways of doing things and thinking about them. Six thousand years of patterning will not be easily changed, and old-paradigm thinkers will fight strenuously, using every spurious argument at their disposal, to defend their old and (seemingly) more comfortable ways of thinking.

> It is difficult to produce a television documentary that is both incisive and probing when every twelve minutes one is interrupted by dancing rabbits singing about toilet paper.
> *Rod Serling*

But as the thirteenth-century Sufi poet Rumi said, "Out beyond ideas of right-doing and wrong-doing there is a field. I'll meet you there." It is important for us to see beyond the rights and wrongs of dualistic thinking—of separateness—and we can do this best by remaining open and listening to the voices of oneness.

We have become quantitatively better at listening to a lot of things: the media, the Internet, news, gossip, advertising, stock prices, data. Over the past 500 years, and during the past 100 in particular, we have sharply accelerated our adeptness at listening to science, reason, rational argument, logic, and analysis. But what have we *stopped* listening to? Our unconscious, our intuition, the myths of our heritage and our times, the mysteries of life, and the magic around us. These voices have largely been lost, because today they are generally considered to be an inferior source of knowing, compared with quantifiable data.

Myth

In his dialogues *Critias* and *Timaeus*, the Greek philosopher Plato (427–347 BC) described a circular island nation that existed more than 11,000 years ago called *Atlantis*. This was the domain of Poseidon, god of the sea. It was populated by talented people of high culture and wealth and was a major center of trade, commerce, and influence. After falling in love with a mortal woman named Cleito, Poseidon created a magnificent hilltop dwelling and surrounded it with water and land for her protection. Atlantis was ruled by their five sets of twin boys. On the central hill were two temples, one of which housed a giant gold statue of Poseidon riding a chariot pulled by winged horses. Here, rulers would discuss laws, dispense judgments, and pay tribute to Poseidon. To facilitate travel, a canal was cut through the island running south to the sea. Elephants roamed the land, and an abundance of herbs, fruits, and animals was generated by two harvests a year. For generations, the people of Atlantis lived peaceful and virtuous lives.

Plato's account was originally derived from Solon (640–560 BC), the wise elder and lawgiver from Athens. While he was visiting the town of Sais on the Nile Delta, Egyptian priests told him of the disappearance of a great island empire. This story passed to Plato from Critias through his great-grandfather, who had discussed the story with Solon. In *Timaeus*, Plato quotes Critias' account of the demise of Atlantis, as told to Solon by one of the Egyptian priests:

> *Now in this island of Atlantis there was a great and wonderful empire which had rule over the whole island and several others, and over parts of the continent...But, there occurred violent earthquakes and floods, and in a single day and night of misfortune...the island of Atlantis...disappeared in the depths of the sea.*

The legend of Atlantis was typical of the many myths that guided early human thinking and decision making. This was the *prescientific* era, and it spanned the better part of 6,000 years. During that era, what we now think of as science did not exist. Instead, we looked elsewhere for guidance. If we needed help in making a decision, we might turn to a *myth*—such as the story of Atlantis—that we had been taught through the generations. These myths were transferred through oral tradition, because few at the time could read or write. Such myths would then form the basis of our belief system and, therefore, of our decision making. In those times, decisions were deeply influenced, indeed often solely determined, by the message and metaphor within the myth.

For an age-old question such as "How did we get here?" there were endless creation-myth answers, all strikingly similar. Most of them shared themes of a void, birth, a flood, good and evil forces, disobedience, life transitions, punishment, banishment, death, and redemption.

Mystery

In this prescientific era, *mystery* was also a common and reassuring source of knowledge, wisdom, and understanding. We were content to treat as mystery how the heavens were formed, or how plants grow, or how thunder develops. Six thousand years ago, we didn't know the scientific answers to these questions, so we just made them up and called them mysteries. Often people didn't even bother to come up with an answer. They simply said it is. There's no need to know.

There are two ways to live your life: one is as though nothing is a miracle; the other is as though everything is a miracle.
Albert Einstein

I am not advocating a return to ignorance, but rather a renewed acceptance of the mysteries of the universe which may allow for greater appreciation of the wonders of the world and the magnificence of self and others. When we approach each moment of our lives as if it were a problem or puzzle to be solved, we sap our mysteries of their essence and deep wisdom.

A friend and I (he was a client at the time) were watching the sun slide below the horizon, the sky daubed with exuberant crimson hues. John is a brilliant, conscious leader, and I was coaching him to listen to myth, mystery, and magic as brilliantly as he did to science, reason, and logic. I asked him, "John, what do you see when you watch a sunset?"

"I see pollution and haze from inversion layers," he replied. "I wonder how far away the horizon is. How long do you think it will take for the sun to sink below the horizon? I often wonder why a bright green dot will appear at that precise moment. I reflect that, as we watch the sun set here, there are people watching it rise at the same moment somewhere on the other side of the Earth, and I wonder where that is and who they are. I wonder how hot the sun is, how many more years the sun will exist. It's very hot, you know—just 0.03 percent of the sunlight that falls on the Earth could provide all the energy we need. And I recall that atomic fusion requires atoms to be heated to temperatures that are four times the heat of the sun's core. Did you know that it would take 109 Earths, side by side, to span the sun?"

I asked him, "John, what you say is so interesting and significant, and yet I wonder if you ever just watch the sun setting and simply meditate and marvel at its beauty? Are you ever simply one with the sun, without analysis or measurement or inquiry?"

Treasuring the mystery of life enables us to be one again—not separate and analytical, but united, observer with the observed. Science is not wrong, but it's just *one* way to see life—myth, mystery, and magic offer additional ways.

Magic

In the prescientific era, we appointed magicians among our tribes and clans—shamans, doctors, and healers, or religious and holy people—to carry the magic. Before making a decision, one would visit a magician, who would make some sort of potion, conduct a ritual or celebration, perform a dance, or perhaps say a prayer or perform a sacrifice. Whatever the challenge—weather, health, fertility, prosperity, or security—a magician would do something to help find the answer to the challenges and questions of the community.

During the prescientific era, people relied on myth, mystery, and magic for decision making and for making their way in the world, considering them universal truths containing the explanations and answers for everything. Sharing these universal stories made us feel as one, and we used them for guidance in gathering the harvest, hunting successfully, selecting a lover, creating families, and choosing our crafts. That's how we reached agreement, formed our impressions, and charted the course of our lives. The comfort of knowing that we shared the same myths, mysteries, and magic made sense of our lives. We were one, and we viewed everything as an integrated whole. A disrespectful act by us to the Earth, for example, was avoided because it might bring forth a similar act directed at ourselves. This is how it was in a world where we instinctively knew we were one.

How We Became Dedicated to Separateness

We can trace the roots of how we interpret and think about life today to the early Greek theorists, especially the pre-Socratic philosophers. They were among the first to reject the traditional mythological explanations, described above, of the phenomena they saw around them, in favor of more rational explanations. They began to use reason and observation to reveal the true nature of the world as they saw it, and they used rational argument to explain and promote their views.

Socrates, generally regarded as the father of ethics, developed a method of inquiry known as the Socratic Method, which is a negative method of hypothesis elimination. Better hypotheses are forced to emerge as those that lead to contradictions are steadily identified and eliminated.

Socrates' student was Plato, who, in turn, taught Aristotle, the last two going on to shape modern Western thinking more than any before them and perhaps since. Aristotle initiated what became known as the scientific method through his concept of "induction," a method of reasoning in which the premises of an argument support the conclusion, but do not ensure it. A simple example of inductive reasoning might go like this: "A billiard ball moves when struck by a cue; therefore, for every force, there is an equal and opposite force."

Then, in the late fifteenth century, the evolution of the scientific method received a critical boost from Niccolò Machiavelli, who initiated an extraordinary new way of thinking by separating politics and ethics. This introduced a radical departure from viewing life as a complete, integrated whole to viewing it in small, discrete parts in order to explain the whole.

You can't disaggregate a myth. You can't pull apart the pieces to see what makes the whole. A myth just is, and mystery and magic are the same.

The path of myth, mystery, and magic is a whole and is complete.

Machiavelli, a minor politician, was banished by the Medicis to his country estate for his republican sympathies. He wrote *The Prince* between 1513 and 1517, though it was not published until 1532. *The Prince* was strongly based on an astute, unsentimental awareness of human nature as flawed and selfish and proved enormously popular with Italian audiences. It was no normal text about protocol or conventional strategy. Rather, it set down a new way of thinking about sovereignties and the acquisition, deployment, and retention of available military, political, and psychological assets, but all without consideration of oneness. His book changed, forever, not only political thought, but also *the very way we think*. Machiavelli wrote:

> *How one lives is so far removed from how one ought to live that he who abandons what one does for what one ought to do, learns rather his own ruin than his preservation.*

In laying out this idea, he departed dramatically from previous political thought by leaving no room for the myth, mystery, and magic that had almost exclusively shaped human thought in the previous millennia. He also introduced the notion that one might behave immorally without consequences, giving a new respectability to the concept of separateness.

In *The Discourses Against Machiavelli*, written in 1576, the French writer Innocent Gentillet described *The Prince* as advocating statecraft by ruthlessness and unprincipled duplicity, and many since him have claimed that it sowed the seeds of French political corruption and a growing amoral approach to sovereignty, politics, and social leadership. This new thinking made a virus-like crossing of the English Channel, spreading across Britain through the works of highly influential contemporary dramatists such as William Shakespeare and Christopher Marlowe. In the prologue to his play *The Jew of Malta* (circa 1589), Marlowe had Machiavelli address the audience summarizing the Elizabethan perception of his thought in this way: "I count religion but a childish toy, / And hold there is no sin but ignorance."

As with all radical and revolutionary ideas, the initial response of those in power was to feel threatened. The Vatican deemed *The Prince* to be so dangerous and pernicious that it was added to the Papal Index of Prohibited Books in 1559. The Vatican was profoundly alarmed by Machiavelli's dangerous challenge to the existing paradigm, which was based on myth, mystery, and magic. What it feared most was that Machiavelli had done something no one had ever done before: he had given people a new, more advanced method of rational thinking. And its fears were justified, for this new thinking was to help accelerate the scientific age and the use of separateness as a legitimate way of reasoning. Indeed, Machiavelli's separateness method of observing people and life helped to reprogram our brains, rewiring, as it were, our biological processes for interpreting life. (I will say more about this process in chapter 3.)

With the introduction of Machiavelli's new way of thinking, people were being encouraged to analyze decisions by breaking them up into discrete, separate parts. He taught that it was possible to make good ethical decisions that were bad from a political perspective, or bad ethical decisions that were good from a political perspective ("good" and "bad" being subjective descriptions, of course).

Machiavelli's writing inspired René Descartes, another important contributor to this radical change in thinking about the world. Descartes, a mathematician and philosopher, used and advanced Machiavelli's new process of reasoning by asserting that unless something could be measured, it was not real. Thus, he invalidated myth, mystery, and magic.

Descartes' theory, and the thinking of the new contemporary scientists, gave rise to the scientific revolution, ushering in the beginnings of the paradigm based on analysis and logic. The scientific revolution completely eclipsed the special nature of myth, mystery, and magic, *and the notion of oneness began its full retreat.*

Science Where None Exists

Our contemporary scientific era has its roots in this earlier transformation. We find ourselves today at a place where science
determines our belief system. If something is logical and rational,
and if it can be analyzed and captured in an equation and charted
on a spread sheet—if it is measurable—then we believe it to be
real. If, on the other hand, something cannot be measured by such
means, or if it can't be defined in some type of
software, pie chart, metric or empirical analysis,
then we deem it to be "touchy-feely," "warm and
fuzzy," or "soft." We may even doubt its existence or consider it dangerous. For example,
although placebos are as effective as drugs in
many cases, this reality is seldom considered in
our mainstream model of healing. Along with the placebo effect,
we continue to ignore the power of oneness and myth, mystery,
and magic, preferring a choice based on what we can measure
"scientifically." Many physicians also dismiss the validity of spontaneous recoveries, because they are unaware that we are partners
with something much larger—oneness.

*This isn't right. It
isn't even wrong.*
Wolfgang Pauli, on a
paper submitted by a
physicist colleague

Some of the greatest thinkers in history followed a path beyond
academic convention. Several researchers have determined that
Albert Einstein's genius had as much to do with his environment
as with his brain capacity. He brought the fresh thinking of an
outcast to his work. As leading Einstein scholar Gerald Holton
puts it, "He comes in entirely as an outsider. He has no stakes at
all in any of the nineteenth- and early twentieth-century physics.
He comes there in his twenties, with a full-time job, and he lets his
mind wander. He's not endangering his academic position,
because he doesn't have one, and he can take those risks."

We have advanced the "science" of rational thinking close to its
limits and may have paid a steep price for it. Sumantra Ghoshal
wrote that many of the "worst excesses of recent management

practices have their roots in a set of ideas that have emerged from business-school academics over the last 30 years."[3] He argues that attempts by business schools, especially Harvard and the Chicago School, to portray human emotions and behavior as business science resembling "a kind of physics" have led to simplistic management theories. These have been posed as grand theorems supported by complex mathematical models and empirical analysis, earning them worldwide respectability (in an age in which science is worshiped) and an aura of deep knowledge, where, in fact, there is none.

Looking at medicine, for example, the "root" of the matter, if you will forgive me, may be summed up this way:

- 1000 BC: Here, eat this root.
- AD 1000: That root is heathen. Say this prayer.
- AD 1800: That prayer is pure superstition. Here, take this potion.
- AD 1940: That potion is snake oil. Here, take this pill.
- AD 1980: That pill is ineffective. Here, take this antibiotic.
- AD 2000: That antibiotic doesn't work. Here, eat this root.

An Internet wit has reminded us that in 1000 BC, we intuitively understood that the root was good for us, because we were one with the Earth. Today, as we realize that wellness is not achieved by pharmaceutical medicine alone, we once again turn to earlier, more natural methods of healing because we now have a deeper understanding of how everything is connected. The difference is that then, we *unconsciously* knew that the root could heal us; today, we *consciously* know so.

Some universities are stirring, becoming more aware of the need to address the whole, rather than the micro-parts of traditional business school curricula.

3. Ghoshal, Sumantra; Academy of Management Learning and Education (v4, n1), March 2005

When I heard the learned astronomer,
When the proofs, the figures, were ranged in columns before me,
When I was shown the charts and diagrams, to add, divide, and measure them,
When I sitting heard the astronomer where he lectured with much applause in the lecture-room,
How soon unaccountable I became tired and sick,
Till rising and gliding out I wandered off by myself,
In the mystical moist night-air, and from time to time,
Looked up in perfect silence at the stars.

Walt Whitman

Both the Harvard Business School and the leading European business school, INSEAD, have concluded from their research that the two most effective new business tools for twenty-first-century executives are meditation and intuition. A similar conclusion has been reached at a growing number of other colleges.

Stanford has established an Institute of Design to teach design thinking and strategy to business, engineering, and design students. The founder of this "D-school" is David Kelley, professor of mechanical engineering in Stanford's product design program and also founder of the famed Palo Alto design firm IDEO. Kelley is following the energy of successful design-centered firms like Target and JetBlue Airways. The Institute of Design at the Illinois Institute of Technology is also leading this new movement in business schools. "More than half our graduates are going into strategy, marketing, and research in companies, not just design," says Patrick Whitney, director of the Institute.

The emergence of design as a new partner in business education signals a promising trend of embracing a holistic, aesthetic view of business, rather than the traditional, narrow silos of specialization. Large consulting companies, such as McKinsey & Co., have certainly noticed, snapping up recent graduates of these programs.

Perhaps we should develop new courses such as "The Responsibility of Business for the Whole," "Honoring the Spirit in Business," "Building Lasting Relationships," "Balancing Logic with Intuition," and "Creating Businesses That Inspire Everyone," so that we can guide those who lead others to embrace the new level of conscious leadership that will be essential for our continued sustainability.

In many industries, change is still slow. For example, in the crazy, mad-hatter's-tea-party world of publishing, few authors secure a contract to publish their book without first submitting a book proposal (a sort of a marketing plan), complete with such information as the demographics of intended readers, the means by which distribution is to be effected, estimates of likely sales, chapter outlines, and sample chapters. What is the result of all this "science"? Of the 195,000 new English-language titles published every year, only 10 percent earn enough to cover the advance on royalties that the publishers gave to the author, and more than one out of three of all hardcover books that publishers edit, print, distribute, and market are returned to publishers, destined for the remainder tables or to be recycled into dishrags!

Exceptions based on oneness are emerging. Berrett-Koehler is a small San Francisco-based publisher with a catalogue featuring just 30 new titles a year. "A lot of publishers treat authors like nuisances," says Steve Piersanti, BK's founder and president. "We treat them like partners"—in other words, as one. Authors are intimately engaged in all the stages of development of the book, which is highly unusual in publishing. The average Berrett-Koehler author sells 15,000 books—27 percent more than the national average, and although Piersanti owns 54 percent of the company, 100 authors, customers, employees, and suppliers own the remaining 46 percent.

Among large publishing houses, Berrett-Koehler stands out as a unique model. In other fields, too, we can find individuals and organizations in pioneering roles. In general, however, we continue to exclude myth, mystery, and magic in favor of relying on science alone—not only preferring separateness over oneness, but often also focusing on the *wrong separate parts*. For example, the United States maintains a research apparatus costing $2 billion annually and employing 10,000 people to measure the nation's well-being. Despite the momentous changes in the makeup of the economy during the past 40 years, no new national statistical measure was instituted until September 2004, when the Quarterly Services Survey was introduced to reflect the growth of information and technology in our society. While the per-capita GDP of America (the value of all goods and services produced, divided by the population) has tripled during the past 50 years, and although the U.S. is the undisputed leader of the world by economic measures, it stands sixteenth out of 65 countries in the world in terms of happiness, according to the World Values Survey. Meanwhile, less advantaged Nigeria, Mexico, Venezuela, El Salvador, and Puerto Rico top the list. A similar survey showed that happiness in Britain peaked in 1976, a time when the country was in the grip of runaway inflation, terrorism, drought, bell bottoms, and punk rock, and the International Monetary Fund was forced to bail the country out.

There is a growing consensus that relying on science alone to measure material wealth in postindustrial societies is, in itself, no longer the best or only way to assess our broader happiness, whether in our communities, organizations, or families. This awareness is causing us to look for something more than just the science and metrics. We want to find something that recognizes our connection to the bigger picture. We want not just a measure of the smallness of our modest lives, but a measure of the oneness of everything to which we are intimately connected.

Science sometimes falls short when we use it alone to try to fathom the separate depths of our essence—our inspiration comes from the oneness of that essence.

Educating for Oneness Thinking

Robert Maynard Hutchins had a well-developed sense of oneness. He became president of the University of Chicago in 1929 at the youthful age of 30. The combination of his relative inexperience and his passion and brilliance led him to change the roles of the presidency and the university. At the time of his inauguration, Chicago was known as a leading research institution, with the undergraduate and graduate programs playing second fiddle to professional writing, research, and publication. Hutchins, with his vision that the university should graduate individuals liberally educated in the great works of the Western world, moved the undergraduate program to the forefront.

In 1952, this man, who proved to be one of the greatest thinkers in the history of U.S. education, wrote a landmark essay promoting the benefits of what he termed a "liberal education." In that essay, *The Great Conversation*, Hutchins contended that the classical works of Western thought constituted one long conversation in which men and women from successive ages told the stories of how they engaged with the myriad problems of humanity. These works, he maintained, should be read as part of an ongoing conversation that enabled a student to construct his or her response to the world in the context of what had been said and done before—our collective journey of oneness.

One of Hutchins' notable legacies was the assembly of 54 books called *The Great Books of the Western World*, a master collection containing the most important ideas, stories, and discoveries produced by Western thinkers and writers from Homer to Freud (a complete set of which still resides in my library).

I grew up with parents who shared Hutchins' philosophy. My mother was a concert pianist and my father a leading engineer. Both wanted me to enjoy the benefits of a classical education: languages, history, the arts, literature, and philosophy. They wanted me to appreciate the oneness of humanity, though I did not see it that way at the time. I studied Greek and Latin at an early age, and read the original texts of ancient myths and legends about gods and goddesses, minotaurs, satyrs, centaurs, serpents, and devils—larger-than-life characters who fought wars, had great love affairs, and created and destroyed dynasties. Thus, I learned about human treachery, love, greed, tragedy, and joy.

I also learned French, and this, together with Greek and Latin, gave me a life-time gift. Few words are a mystery to me today—their meaning can be found in the roots of a word from one of these languages. Later, my family moved to Argentina. I attended a boarding school there for five years, where all lessons were in Spanish. Many years later, as the CEO of Manpower Limited, I oversaw businesses in both French- and English-speaking countries, working daily with bilingual teams.

I am grateful every day that I was not encouraged to study a single narrow discipline, because what I learned has been immeasurably more helpful in guiding and leading organizations and understanding the oneness of people and life.

For many leaders, running an organization has been distilled to a mundane pattern of meeting the numbers and the metrics every quarter, and this tends to be how the organization's success and the skills of its management are defined. For many, it defines who we are. In *The Little Prince,* Antoine de Saint-Exupéry wrote:

> *Grown-ups like numbers. When you tell them about a new friend, they never ask questions about what really matters. They never ask: "What does his voice sound like?" "What games does he like best?" "Does he collect butterflies?" They ask: "How old is he?" "How many brothers does he have?" "How much does he weigh?" "How much money does his father make?" Only then do they think they know him.*

> *If you tell grown-ups, "I saw a beautiful red brick house, with geraniums at the windows and doves on the roof," they won't be able to imagine such a house. You have to tell them, "I saw a house worth a hundred thousand dollars." Then they exclaim, "What a pretty house!"*

Blending Atomism with Holism

None of this is to deny the incredible fruits of science that make our day-to-day lives so much more enjoyable than they would otherwise be. Rather, I am proposing that we *also* make room in our lives and our thinking for the return of myth, mystery, and magic; that we take the very best of science and use it to help us achieve a better appreciation of our oneness.

Quantification alone cannot inspire people; it does not create the magic we are looking for. People are much more than robots that go to work to make their numbers every day, based on a pseudo-scientific theorem of rational, self-interested, utility-maximizing, shareholder-pleasing *homo economicus*.

The "let's-measure-everything" approach cannot, on its own, lift our hearts or spirits. On the contrary, it can weigh us down. It can put a heaviness into our awareness and an urgent inner knowing that all this is, in many ways, artificial and shallow. At some stage in our lives—even if only on our deathbeds—most of us will come to realize that there is more to life than breaking down our activities into the separateness of numbers that must be met each quarter. Somewhere, most of us believe at an inner level of knowing, there is something bigger, some myth, mystery, or magic that connects us to a larger whole—oneness.

Of course, running an organization—or any community of people for that matter—and being a responsible leader, requires us to pay attention to the numbers and to act prudently on the information revealed by the metrics. But we can grow our successes by consciously leading organizations with a greater awareness of the importance of myth, mystery, and magic. This is what inspires the people who work there, because inspired people have a way of making their numbers. But that's not the *only* point of the exercise, and this is where the greatest potential for inspiring, conscious leadership lies. We are yearning to find our way again and become attached once more to what is real and what stirs our spirits in contemporary organizations and life. We want to move beyond relying *only* on science or the measurable to the feeling of oneness that comes from also embracing myth, mystery, and magic.

And whenever we insist on measuring, we need to be sure that we are measuring the right thing and using the right tools with which to measure—and these may often be our hearts, rather than our heads.

For more than 20 years, Professor Edwin R. Keedy of the University of Pennsylvania Law School began the first class of his courses by putting two figures on the blackboard: 4 and 2. Then he would ask, "What's the solution?"

One student would call out "six." Another would say "two." Then someone would shout "eight!" But Professor Keedy would shake his head as he pointed out their collective error. "You all are so quick with an answer, but all of you failed to ask the vital question: What is the problem? Unless you know what the problem is, you cannot possibly find the answer."

Bernard Baruch, the American financier and presidential advisor, said, "If all you have is a hammer, everything looks like a nail." Metrics are like that. My friend John could very easily have developed a brilliant sunset formula during our sunset conversation. But great leaders include and transcend these limiting impulses. They have a holistic approach to life and work, one that encompasses both science and the ability to measure things on the one hand and the capacity and willingness to appreciate myth, mystery, and magic, and the values they hold for us, on the other. This pragmatic holism is one of the reasons that leadership is so difficult to teach and that context is so vital for understanding great leadership and the effectiveness of an inspiring, conscious leader.

3

ONENESS REGAINED

O RACLE CORP.'S HOSTILE takeover attempt of PeopleSoft in 2003 created a brushfire of rumors suggesting that more than half of the target corporation's employees could be laid off after the merger. Employees began to look for work elsewhere, and relationships got nasty.

In June 2003, Craig Conway, then the CEO of PeopleSoft, said that Oracle's takeover bid was like "someone offering to buy your pet dog, only to take him around the back, and shoot him."

Oracle CEO Larry Ellison responded by observing that if he ever met Conway and his dog and only had one bullet in his gun, "the bullet would not be for the dog."

At the next PeopleSoft conference, Conway appeared wearing a bulletproof vest and accompanied by his dog, Abbey.

A year later, Conway was replaced with PeopleSoft's founder, the unconventional, Hawaiian-shirt-clad Dave Duffield, who immediately issued an e-mail to employees. "It's great to be back," he wrote. "For those of you who don't know me, you can expect to see me in the halls, on the road, in the cafeterias, looking for feedback and the opportunity to meet you."

Duffield didn't bring just science to this party. He also brought back the myth, mystery, and magic of the founder. He recognized the need to shore up morale and make the organization and its

people whole again. He quickly introduced a plan to be activated if
another company acquired control of PeopleSoft and fired its staff,
providing employees with between 150 and 200 percent of their
annual salary and bonus, plus up to two years of health coverage.
According to Lynn Bersch, a partner at the law firm Reed Smith,
which specializes in employment issues, PeopleSoft's packages were
an "extraordinary measure." Bersch describes the uncertainty of a
hostile takeover as "a big deal when your livelihood depends on it.
You don't want to be the last employee standing."

Many businesses have change-of-control clauses for executives,
but few deploy such benefits to all their employees. Duffield saw
the need to identify the immeasurable issues of the human spirit—
the aching hearts and insecurities of people—and deal with them.
He represented the myth, mystery, and magic of a larger-than-life
visionary who had, from the very beginning, seen the centrality of
people by calling his company PeopleSoft.[4]

> There's no business like show business, but there are several businesses like accounting.
> *David Letterman*

Changes are in the air. The failures of Enron,
Arthur Andersen, Parmalat, and MCI may
represent the last death throes of a former era.
Jeffrey Immelt, chairman and CEO of GE, one
of America's most admired companies, has said,
"The reason people come to work for GE is that
they want to be about something that is bigger
than themselves. People want to work hard, they
want to get promoted, they want stock options. But they also want
to work for a company that is making a difference, a company that
is doing great things in the world."

---

4. Five thousand layoffs occurred shortly after the takeover anyway—Duffield was
unable to sustain the employees' inspiration. The new, combined company's CEO,
Larry Ellison, speaking on CNBC in a TV interview, matter-of-factly observed,
"We never like to be in the position where we have more employees than jobs—
but that's just one of the things that happen when you glue two big companies
together." He added, with more science than magic, "We're sorry." Dave Duffield
offered $10,000 of his own money to every employee receiving a pink slip making
less than $150,000 a year.

The Zen Master's Clothes

A Zen Master lived the simplest kind of life in a little hut at the foot of a mountain. One evening, while he was away, a thief sneaked into the hut, only to find there was nothing in it to steal. The Zen Master returned and found him.

"You have come a long way to visit me," he told the prowler, "and you should not return empty-handed. Please take my clothes as a gift."

The thief was bewildered, but he took the clothes and ran away.

The Master sat naked, watching the moon. "Poor fellow," he mused. "I wish I could give him this beautiful moon."

Everything that occurs can be reframed from separateness to oneness. There are no actions without consequences, Machiavelli's assertions notwithstanding. When we fail to understand this, neglecting to see life as a whole, we invite incidents that seem to emanate from another place, such as 9/11. But these events don't just happen. They occur because we are entwined in a whole system. They are cries from one part of us to another part of us out of a deep desire to become whole. We are one.

Of course, there is no single version of the truth, one valid opinion, one right view, one correct answer, one right approach, or even one absolute faith. As James Barrie said, "I am not young enough to know everything." There is always another angle, and this is what makes the whole. A delicacy to one is disgusting to another; a person of faith to one is an infidel to another. A beautiful painting to one is an enigma to another. The *yin* and the *yang* make up the whole.

As conscious leaders, we become whole when we see that our focused, singular commitment to making the numbers and the metrics cannot be effective on its own, but only when it is part of the whole picture—only when we see that it takes more than metrics to make up the whole.

Oneness: The Way Forward

Science *and* myth, mystery, and magic explain life. On its own, science cannot explain the beauty of a sunset. It cannot explain falling in love, or a great joke, or the soft smell of a newborn baby. It may offer a technical explanation, but it cannot explain the *experience*. You can try to explain to me on a spreadsheet what a new baby smells like, but I won't *feel* what you mean. Similarly, you might write a description for me of falling in love, or making love. I could read what you wrote and understand the definition. I might even see a picture or a movie that describes it another way. But the only way I can feel *and* know what it is like is to *experience* it myself. The same applies to other life events, such as the taste of a good wine or a fabulous meal, or the experience of friends.

These things are beyond measure, involving a serenity and a sense of peaceful integration with a larger purpose. Perhaps that is what Henry David Thoreau had in mind when he wrote, "When I hear music, I fear no danger. I am invulnerable. I see no foe. I am related to the earliest times, and to the latest." Science cannot explain these experiences, yet they are all a part of life. Indeed, some would say they are much more a part of life than other things.

Einstein said, "I did not discover the Theory of Relativity by rational thinking alone." He discovered it imagining himself riding on sunbeams while daydreaming in a field one day. He wondered what it would be like to travel on those sunbeams without the restrictions of space and time. Falling asleep, he had a dream that led to the discovery of his great theory. Thus, this discovery, from one of the greatest thinkers of our time, didn't come from science. It came from a dream, from the realm of myth, mystery, and magic. Einstein also said, "The more I study physics, the more I am drawn to metaphysics."

In our linear, exclusive, science-based thinking, we give too little credibility and value to relating, inspiring, and leading through myth, mystery, and magic—through the broader perspective of oneness. We can grow and achieve potential even beyond our fantasies if we acknowledge that greatness of all kinds, including major scientific discoveries, as Einstein has shown us, can come from dreams and from myth, mystery, and magic—when we see, and understand, our connection, not just to the separate parts, but also to the oneness of life.

The awareness that we are not separate, that we do not live in a world of discrete people, organizations, lands, nations, things, or feelings, is the single most important step toward transforming our world. It is this awareness that so many have been yearning to see in our leaders, colleagues, friends, and families. And it is this awareness that will make the inspiring difference in our lives, our work, and our world.

Being a Ten Percenter

Research by Michael Merzenich, a leading neuroscientist from the University of California at San Francisco, has shown that after 100 times, a laboratory rat can solve a puzzle perfectly every time. After 200 times, it will remember how to solve the puzzle for the rest of its life. The rat gains expertise and mastery not from intuition, but through the permanent rewiring of its brain.

MRI scanners can measure a similar effect in humans who have perfected a skill—flute players, for example, who have strengthened the brain areas that control the fingers, tongue, and lips. Everyday tasks, such as how we squeeze a tube of toothpaste, ride a bicycle, or select our diet, all result in similar, permanent changes to the brain. These modifications become deeply embedded, and it requires significant effort for most people to change them. For example, according to Raphael Levey, founder of the Global Medical Forum, 80 percent of the staggering $2 trillion spent in America's health-care system each year is the result of five behavioral issues: smoking; overindulging in alcohol; overeating and poor diet; stress; and inadequate exercise. Research showing how these five habits lead to disease and death is incontrovertible and widely available and communicated.

Yet, explains Edward Miller, dean of the Medical School and CEO of the hospital at Johns Hopkins University, 600,000 Americans have heart-bypass surgery and 1.3 million more have angioplasties annually, costing some $30 billion. Although these procedures ease chest pains, they do little to prevent heart attacks or prolong life. Half the bypass grafts clog up in a few years, and half the angioplasties after a few months.

Says Miller, "If you look at people after coronary-artery bypass grafting two years later, 90 percent of them have not changed their lifestyle. And that's been studied over and over and over again. And so we're missing some link there. Even though they know they have a very bad disease and they know they should change their lifestyle, for whatever reason, they can't."

Old ideas based on separation have been similarly hardwired into our brains, making it very difficult to change. It is astonishing, for example, that for more than 30 years, the U.S. airline industry has watched Southwest Airlines grow and prosper using a business model that is entirely different from its own. Other airlines have stuck stubbornly to the old model, even while sinking into bankruptcy. None has realized that converting their entire businesses to become more like Southwest would have enabled them to survive. It took 24 years before just one other airline, JetBlue, emerged to follow the Southwest approach, and it was a start-up, not an established airline. Southwest Airlines now enjoys 10 percent of the airline market and is the nation's sixth biggest airline.

This book is about how to inspire the world to share the views of the ten-percenters, starting with the most difficult step— ourselves. It is about recognizing the lack of potential in a broken paradigm and the possibilities of a new one, difficult though it is to let go of a comfortable but worn-out worldview and accept a new one, and difficult though it is to rewire our brains as we move from separateness to oneness. If we accept the logic, then do the work, we can become the pioneers who will grow the 10 percent to 100 percent and thereby change the world.

When someone says to us, "I like your ideas, but let's be realistic... *they* will never change," referring to others in their organizations who are at more senior levels, it is usually code for "I do not want to change." When this happens, we are presented with a personal fork in the road. One path leads to the 90 percent, and the other to the 10 percent. The choice is ours.

Part Two of this book describes how we can choose to live in the 10 percent, how we can shift the way we live our lives, engage in our relationships with others, and consciously lead and inspire them and our organizations by reaching beyond rational thinking alone, by embracing the whole, by understanding that we are one—not separate—by blending rational thinking with myth, mystery, and magic.

Why, then, have to be human?

Oh, not because happiness exists,

Nor out of curiosity...

But because being here means so much;

Because everything here,

Vanishing so quickly, seems to need us,

And strangely keeps calling to us...

To have been

Here once, completely, even if only once,

To have been at one with the earth—

This is beyond undoing.

Rainer Maria Rilke, 1875–1926
German author and poet

PART TWO

The Practice of Oneness

Students achieving Oneness
will move on to Twoness.
Woody Allen

4

4

THE CASTLE PRINCIPLES

THE QUESTION, OF COURSE, is, *How* are we to realize oneness? How are we to lead our lives, in any context and in any role, so that we contribute to the whole? One of the ways by which this can be achieved is through the CASTLE Principles, which are the result of extensive field-testing, both formal and informal, of my theories and findings regarding how successful people and companies actually do things.[5]

CASTLE is an acronym for six principles of being and action that have proven, and are proving, to bring oneness to many lives:

---

5. Please see my book *Inspire! What Great Leaders Do* (John Wiley & Sons, 2004) for more details of the successful implementation, by many organizations and individuals, of *Higher Ground Leadership*®, particularly the foreword written by 15 CEOs who describe their personal experiences (http://www.secretan.com/inspire).

Courage: Being brave enough to reach beyond the boundaries created by our existing, often deeply held, limitations, fears, and beliefs. Initiating change in our lives, of any kind, is only possible when we are courageous enough to take the necessary action.

Authenticity: Committing oneself to showing up and being fully present in all aspects of life. Removing the mask and becoming a real, vulnerable, and intimate human being, a person without self-absorption who is genuine and emotionally and spiritually connected to others.

Service: Focusing on the needs of others by listening to them, identifying their needs, and meeting them. Being inspiring, rather than following a self-focused, competitive, fear-based approach.

Truthfulness: Being truthful in all thoughts, words, and actions, and listening openly to the truth of others and refusing to compromise integrity or to deny obvious or universal truths, even when avoiding the truth might, on the face of it, seem easier, especially in testing times.

Love: Embracing the underlying oneness with others and life. Relating to and inspiring others and touching their hearts in ways that add to who you both are as persons.

Effectiveness: Being capable of, and successful in, achieving the physical, material, intellectual, emotional, and spiritual goals we set in life.

The CASTLE Principles in Action

The CASTLE Principles are a theory of life. But they are more than that. They are practical and pragmatic ways to live.

Frank Stronach was born in the small town of Weiz in the foothills of the Austrian Alps and grew up in a gritty neighborhood oppressed by war and depression. Leaving school at the age of 14, he apprenticed as a tool- and diemaker. Keen to travel the world, he arrived in Montreal in 1954 and then traveled by bus to Kitchener, Ontario, where he found a job as a dishwasher in a local hospital. While there, he saved enough money to move to Toronto to look for work as a toolmaker.

In 1957, using his personal savings and a $1,000 overdraft, young Frank purchased secondhand lathes and milling machines to set up shop in a rented gatehouse in Toronto's old manufacturing district. Here, working long hours, spending the night on a cot next to his lathe, Frank began building his small operation, growing it from ten employees into the world's largest automotive parts manufacturer, $20-billion Magna International.

Half a century later, Hurricane Katrina lashed New Orleans with fierce winds and floods, displacing 750,000 people. It was the worst natural disaster in U.S. history. The majority of those affected lost their homes, and many were threatened by hunger and disease, particularly the elderly and the very poor. Help was slow to come, and the magnitude of the devastation seemed to overwhelm the relief agencies, making poorly organized relief efforts appear futile and inadequate.

Frank Stronach, 73 by now, decided to step in and put his company's resources, organizational expertise, and strong community spirit to work to help the victims of Katrina. Recalling his own penniless days as a new immigrant to Canada, he knew how it felt to be desperately poor and hungry. "Those things are burned right into your soul," he said. He realized that quick, courageous action was needed.

"The great thing about a large company that makes a profit is that you have the capability to jump in and be helpful, right away," said Stronach.

In other words, there are always opportunities to serve.

In less than five days following Katrina's furious landfall, Stronach assembled a small team of Magna executives to direct efforts to transport victims of the hurricane out of New Orleans and take them to Magna's MEC Palm Meadows thoroughbred horse-training facility near West Palm Beach, Florida. The facility provides accommodation for some 400 people, offering rooms equipped with beds, refrigerators, microwave ovens, and bathrooms. There is also a commissary, a cafeteria, and a recreation area.

Chartering buses and working with the U.S. Army, FEMA, and the American Red Cross, the Magna team successfully evacuated 250 people from New Orleans to Palm Meadows within 36 hours, demonstrating effectiveness long before federal and state services were able to initiate relief efforts. The MEC facility provided comfortable shelter and accommodation for the hurricane victims.

But Stronach knew that his service to the community couldn't stop there. More needed to be done, and he wanted to be even more effective. Many families with small children, seniors, and disabled people were among the evacuees.

"Helping people, feeding and shelter, that's the easy part," he says. "The challenging part is what to do to get them back on their feet again."

Magna acquired 1,000 acres of land in the small town of Simmesport, Louisiana, and built 49 three-bedroom 1,300 square-foot houses and other infrastructure that would allow the families left homeless by the hurricane to begin rebuilding their lives. Stronach wanted his company's quick, effective action in helping Katrina's victims to inspire other successful corporations to respond similarly to this and other situations. "We create a role model," he said, "and, hopefully, other companies will see what can be done." Toronto-based Giffels/NORR responded by donating its design services to the project.

Dubbed "Canadaville," the Simmesport development included plans for an organic farm for growing vegetables and raising chicken, hogs, and cattle. Stronach was confident that the evacuees would learn to be effective farmers and help the farm become profitable. He made a $10 million, five-year commitment to carry the costs for water, sewage, and upgrades to the Simmesport project's infrastructure. He also funded the employment of three additional police officers and the purchase of two new police cruisers for the town of 1,200.

How did the Simmesport community respond to Canadaville? It was a hard sell, according to Magna official Dennis Mills, because local residents feared turbulence and lawlessness from their new neighbors—the type of behavior they had seen on TV following the flooding in New Orleans. But the prospects of economic benefits flowing to the community eventually convinced the majority of the five-member town council to support the initiative.

Simmesport Mayor James Fontenot was not surprised at the initial resistance. "Anytime you do something different," he said, "there's going to be a group of people against something. We're just trying to prove to them that this will work."

Even Stronach himself was eyed with a certain amount of skepticism by the Simmesport residents and the evacuees alike. Why did he do what he did? What was his ulterior motive? "I kept wondering what he was getting out of this," said new Simmesport resident Allen Wyman, formerly of New Orleans. "I found out he's just a good guy." In other words, Stronach's intentions proved courageous, authentic, serving, truthful, loving and, of course, highly effective—Stronach was *living* the CASTLE Principles and in doing so, inspired others by being one with them.

One of the reasons Magna International was able to help so quickly and effectively is the result of another of Stronach's visions, a corporate culture known as Fair Enterprise. This program guarantees the rights of employees, management, and investors to share in the profits they help produce, and gives employees and managers ownership in the company. This courageous departure from traditional corporate ways involves a truthful sharing of information and a deep desire to serve colleagues through fairness and equity. This "success formula" has helped Stronach build his business into the world's largest and most diversified supplier of automotive components, systems, and modules.

Today, the company's ongoing effectiveness not only generates the profits—its economic permission[6]—to continue to be successful and serve its large international customer base, but also to keep giving back to the community near and far, locally and globally.

In the following chapters, we will explore each of the six CASTLE Principles. I hope they will inspire you, as they take on cumulative momentum for you to grow your own practice of oneness and thus grow your commitment to conscious leadership.

---

6. See "Effectiveness as Economic Permission," in chapter 10 for a full description of this concept.

5

COURAGE

A TRAVELER TOOK HER faithful pet dachshund, Wienie, on an African photo safari. One day, walking at the forest's edge, Wienie was fascinated by some butterflies, which he began to chase. Before long, he was first distracted, and then lost.

Act boldly and unseen forces will come to your aid.
Dorothea Brande

While searching for a way out of the jungle, Wienie noticed a leopard slinking menacingly in his direction, looking very much like he had found lunch. Wienie thought to himself, "Oh! Oh! This is not good!"

Noticing some bones lying on the ground nearby, Wienie immediately settled down to chew on them, with his back to the approaching cat. Just before the leopard pounced on him, the dachshund exclaimed loudly, "Boy, that was one delicious leopard. I wonder if there are any more around here?"

Hearing this, the leopard stopped in his tracks. Reconsidering his intended attack, he slunk quietly into the trees, his heart pounding.

"Whew," said the leopard. "That was close. That dachshund nearly had me."

Meanwhile, a cunning monkey observing this drama from a perch in a nearby tree decided that he could put the dachshund's trickery to good use. The monkey raced off to make a deal with the leopard, but Wienie noticed his speedy departure and suspected this might lead to more trouble.

The monkey caught up with the leopard, explaining breathlessly what he had seen and struck a deal for himself with the leopard. The leopard, furious at being duped, growled, "Here, monkey, hop on my back and let's go and pay a visit to that conniving canine."

Meanwhile, Wienie was trying to find a path out of the jungle, when he noticed the leopard approaching again, this time with the monkey on his back. Wienie thought, "Oh! Oh! What am I going to do now?"

Realizing that escape was really not possible, he sat down with his back to the approaching marauders, pretending that he hadn't noticed them. As soon as they were both within earshot, he said, "Where is that monkey? I sent him off over an hour ago to bring me another leopard."

As Emerson said, "What a new face courage puts on everything!"

Courage Is the Beginning of All Greatness

The first step required for any bold action or idea is courage, because without it, nothing else can happen, especially not anything new, daring, different, contrary, challenging, or innovative. It takes courage to be a ten-percenter.

It takes courage to have an independent thought—to get out of our boxes, our paradigms. It takes courage to become open to new thinking and to be accepting of ideas that do not currently align with our own. It takes courage to be willing to consider that the world could be larger than we imagine it to be, to consider that we are all part of an interdependent whole that does not end

> Daring ideas are like chess men moved forward. They may be beaten, but they may start a winning game.
> *Johann Wolfgang von Goethe*

with us, with our family, with the company we work for, or even with a border between nations. It takes courage to embrace a new awareness that every action we take affects the whole.

It takes courage to come up with a new idea and state it, pioneer it, and implement it. It takes courage to say—in an inspiring way, of course—that we disagree with a decision, a policy, or a strategy. The failure of hundreds of companies could have been averted with a few courageous words that questioned, challenged, opposed, or proposed an alternative to the status quo or the consensus of the herd. We show courage when we introduce a new way of doing anything: a new way of running a company; a new way of leading; a new way of conducting a meeting; a new way of running advertising campaigns; a new way of hiring and selecting people; a new way of retaining or paying them; a new way to lead a country.

It is a blessed thing that in every age someone has had enough individuality and courage to stand by his own convictions.
Robert G. Ingersoll

It takes courage to speak out, to challenge conformity and tradition; to go first and weather the attacks, ridicule, and criticisms of others; to be different. It takes courage to be free, to claim our voice, to own our power, to let the world hear the music inside us.

It takes courage to realize that we are in a rut and that we need to break away from the pack and stride in a new, inspiring, and energizing direction.

It takes a courageous leader to realize that the success of his or her company can't stand on its own because, if one company fails due to the success of another, the marketplace suffers a loss and becomes less as a result—because we are one. Who wins in such a situation? Who wins when we end up in a monopoly because we've knocked everyone else out of business? In the end, this is bullying, the act of a coward, and this sort of success does not benefit us, because it hurts the whole.

How We Lose Our Courage:
The Need for Love and Approval

Why is true courage so hard to find? We are all born with ample courage and almost no fear, but as our lives progress, the ratios reverse. As infants, whatever we want, we cry for, without fear of consequences. We are courageous because we are one with the world—no separation exists in our minds or hearts to make us afraid. Little by little, though, we trade our courage and our wholeness for approval.

The greatest of all human needs is for love and approval. If we choose not to conform to the needs of someone who threatens us by withholding their love and approval, we are faced with a choice: to maintain our courage and personal power, or to lose it. Like Tweedledum in Lewis Carroll's *Alice Through the Looking Glass*, who observed, "I am very brave generally, only today I happen to have a headache," the loss of our courage leads to the loss of our personal power.

> Courage is not the absence of fear, but rather the judgment that something else is more important than fear.
>
> *Ambrose Redmoon*

It starts in small, insidious ways. As children, we quickly learn induced responses: the required behavior that will please those upon whom we depend who threaten to withdraw nourishment, comfort, or affection as "punishment" unless certain ways of behavior are forthcoming. This is how we are "trained," how we are raised, and before long, this becomes the auto-response hardwired into our brains. The English psychoanalyst Donald Winnicott (1896–1971) wrote about the accrued potential harm to developing children when compliance is enforced. In his book *Maturational Processes and the Facilitating Environment: Studies in the Theory of Emotional Development* (International Universities Press, 1965), he says, "Compliance brings immediate rewards, and adults only too easily mistake compliance for growth."

Winnicott felt that compliance promotes the development of a "false self" because the "true self" is not allowed to flourish. Induced responses at the preverbal stage, according to Winnicott, would preclude the emergence of the child's "spontaneous gesture." Ultimately, we transfer what we have learned—avoiding spontaneity—into the rest of our lives, including school, religion, relationships, work, and politics. Lacking the courage to be spontaneous, we begin to live inauthentic lives. Through this conditioning, which, ironically, is spurred by our hunger for oneness, we slowly but systematically lose our courage. Yet, because this happens so gradually, we remain largely unaware of the loss and the separation from our oneness with the world. By now it feels so familiar, and it elicits the approval we yearn for.

If someone suggested that we lacked courage, most of us would disagree. We are convinced that we respond courageously to most of life's situations. But if we look more closely at different areas of our lives—how we communicate; how we relate; how we exchange information; what we wear; what we think; what we say; even how we vote—we can see that these are all areas where we may not always be our authentic selves because of our lack of courage. And when we begin to think about these decision areas of our lives, it becomes clear that there are many moments when we trade wholeness for approval.

In her book *Sacred Contracts: Awakening Your Divine Potential* (Harmony, 2002), Caroline Myss writes, "When you do not seek or need external approval, you are at your most powerful. Nobody can disempower you emotionally or psychologically...You cannot live for prolonged periods of time within the polarity of being true to yourself and needing the approval of others."

When we lack courage, we separate ourselves from our values and beliefs, acting in ways that are incongruent with our feelings. Thus, we become disconnected from our sense of wholeness—our personal oneness. Letting go of the constant craving for approval is one of the essential first steps for reclaiming our courage and, therefore, the sense of personal oneness that is so vital to our fulfillment and inspiration.

Courage and the Need to Tame Our Egos

It takes courage to accept and embrace concepts that, at first blush, may feel counterintuitive because they may not be a part of our current, accumulated awareness. If this were not so, then dysfunctional behavior would not exist. We would always meet the needs of employees and customers, marriages would last forever, and there would be peace on earth. Or, as Dorothy Parker facetiously said,

> Oh, life is a glorious cycle of song,
> A medley of extemporanea;
> And love is a thing that can never go wrong;
> And I am Marie of Romania.

It takes courage to take action based on an idea or concept that does not seem to fit comfortably within our existing worldview. The courage to accept that things, ideas, and people with whom we disagree or who challenge our egos are so often the teachers we need. As the Dalai Lama has said, "Our greatest teachers are our enemies." If we look at each challenge as an opportunity to learn and grow, then we can reframe our relationships, ideas, and actions and reactions—and this takes courage.

Speak your mind, even if your voice shakes.
Maggie Kuhn

I have one of the best occupations imaginable. I work with wonderful, interesting, and brilliant people who genuinely love their work and live the principles of oneness as they inspire and change the world. And yet in my work, I'm constantly faced with the need for courage. I am a veritable lamppost against which many critics raise their legs. I've been

Failure is unimportant. It takes courage to make a fool of yourself.
Charlie Chaplin

challenged every which way by all kinds of people at various stages of my work, and I've been ridiculed for proposing theories of leadership based on courage, authenticity, service, truth, love, and effectiveness. It takes courage, especially in a corporate setting, to stand up and say that if we understood the nature of oneness, loved each other, told the truth, and embraced myth, mystery, and magic, then we would create a more inspiring world. It takes courage because I am also aware that there are many people who depend on me for employment and corporate and personal success, and that if I fail, I am, in some measure, possibly failing them.

So, I need courage to be authentic, to always be who I really am, and to say what I really believe, while also being open to possibilities and ideas other than those that engage my passion. This is where it all begins: finding the courage to break out of the paradigm and the patterns, to say to a board of directors (as a client of mine so courageously did): "I know you want these numbers met by the next quarter, but, quite honestly, I can't do that, because it will hurt people, and we must first honor the human spirit and then the bottom line. So, please give me more time" (which they did because the board was so impressed with the passion and courage of this CEO).

Don't be afraid to go out on a limb. That's where the fruit is.
Anonymous

Recently, I was working closely with a group of 30 CEOs from a large organization. I was guiding them in how to build an inspiring corporate culture by communicating from their souls to the souls of their employees, vendors, and customers. After I had finished presenting my thoughts, one of them, dismissing my ideas out of hand, turned to me and let loose a vituperative volley of criticism wrapped in sarcasm and personal denigration. Having fully ventilated his views, he sat down.

Floored and wounded, I took some deep breaths. The future of my relationship with this company rested on this moment. But so did the future of *their* company. They had an opportunity to grow and become brilliant and inspiring, or to stay stuck in mediocrity, demoralizing leadership, and financial failure. I looked at my intimidator. Thirty faces turned to me, and the air was still as everyone stopped breathing.

> Wherever you see a successful business, someone once made a courageous decision.
>
> *Peter F. Drucker*

"Tom," I said quietly, "I appreciate what you are trying to say, but I wonder if you could say it again in a way that is inspiring?"

Deafening silence. Slowly, everyone let out their breath. A successful teaching moment had occurred in which we had learned something together about courage, communication, and inspiration. This organization has since become one of our most successful clients and gained a national reputation as a brilliant turnaround case study—and Tom has become my skiing buddy.

Courage is a noble quality that leads to growth and authenticity, and it usually leads to something greater than the mere satisfaction of our fear-based egos. Tim Berners-Lee might have been the richest person in the world today if he had been a coward. In 1980, while working at Cern, the European Organization for Research near Geneva, he became frustrated with the difficulty of tracking the projects and the many computers used to analyze scientific experiments. He developed a system for extending virtual memory links, initially between the 5,000 researchers, but eventually to any computer anywhere. In part, this breakthrough ultimately became the World Wide Web.

> Cowardice asks the question—is it safe? Expediency asks the question—is it politic? Vanity asks the question— is it popular? But conscience asks the question—is it right? And there comes a time when one must take a position that is neither safe, nor politic, nor popular; but one must take it because it is right.
>
> *Martin Luther King Jr.*

In 1990, at the age of 35, Berners-Lee chose not to patent his Web software because he was concerned that a Web based on proprietary software could lead to multiple competing Webs owned by large corporations: digital silos of Babel instead of the fluid, seamless system that exists today. He had the courage to listen to his conscience and act responsibly, changing the world by connecting everyone with a computer to everyone else with one, rather than creating a personal fortune. With great courage, he chose to honor oneness, rather than the separate parts, which might have been more expedient and self-serving, but far less fulfilling.[7]

Being Courageous, More Than Talking About It

Courage is important in every aspect of our lives: at work, at school, with our children, in our relationships, as coaches and mentors, in politics. This is where great leadership starts, both in organizational settings and in personal and home environments.

Organizational leadership can't be separated from the rest of life—it is one. There is no "organizational leadership," there is just *leadership*, the best of which is conscious and inspiring and is sourced from the passionate awareness of being one with those whom we lead.

Sorious Samura grew up as one of nine children in a poor family in Freetown, Sierra Leone. While attending an English-speaking Christian school, he learned that drama was an effective method of communicating messages about the political plight of his country. When he was working as an assistant theater manager in the late 1980s, he found a digital video camera and taught

---

7. Tim Berners-Lee now holds the 3Com Founders chair at the Laboratory for Computer Science and Artificial Intelligence Lab (CSAIL) at the Massachusetts Institute of Technology (MIT). He directs the World Wide Web Consortium, an open forum of companies and organizations with the mission to lead the Web to its full potential.

himself to use it, becoming a researcher for Cine Africa. With professional crews from abroad, he later worked on three documentary films for UNICEF Freetown and produced the ten-minute documentary *Giving Them a Chance.*

In 1999, he was filming the rebels who had invaded Freetown, when he was captured, punished, and let off with the warning that if he was caught filming the rebels again, they would kill him. The soldiers threatened to cut out his heart and eat it. Samura, now an acclaimed documentary filmmaker living in London, said, "And they would do it."

Samura was lucky, for few survive capture by the rebels, and none without mementos of scars or loss of limb. Courageously, he immediately returned to the streets, hiding behind windows, dodging sniper fire, filming people dying in flaming buildings, terrified crowds, the tragedy of the torture of a 14-year-old boy, victims blasted by bullets in the crossfire, and fighters having their stomachs or heads shredded by high-velocity bullets. His footage was so disturbing that he was unable to watch it himself back home. Despite the difficulty of being a witness to such horror and pain, he continued to film, keeping his camera hidden, while always trying to keep it steady.

Samura's debut film, *Out of Africa (Cry Freetown),* a harrowing account of the victims of civil war in his country, won a prestigious Rory Peck Award. At the awards ceremony, Samura said, "You guys are clapping me for showing you pictures of my people killing each other. But where were you? Why didn't you go there? I didn't put my life on the line for an award or money. Take your award back if you want to, but go there, go to Sierra Leone."

He received a standing ovation.

How many business or organizational meetings have we suffered through where we have

> Trust that still, small voice that says, "This might work and I'll try it."
>
> *Diane Mariechild*

> Courage is the first of human qualities because it is the quality which guarantees the others.
>
> *Aristotle*

asked under our breath, "Where were you? Why didn't you go there?" How many times have you wondered, "Where were you? Why didn't you go there?"

Courage is the capacity to confirm what can be imagined.
Leo Rosten

Because we so often associate courage with bravery in combat and similar situations, we don't easily recognize the subtler, deeper forms of courage: not the courage that arises from a need to prove one's strength and victory over others, but the courage that enables us to be authentic and truthful, reveal or expose our vulnerability or admit our mistakes, or introduce a novel idea that might be ridiculed at first—even the courage, sometimes, just to say "sorry."

Charles Swindoll has written, "Courage is not limited to the battlefield or the Indianapolis 500 or bravely catching a thief in your house. The real tests of courage are much quieter. They are the inner tests, like remaining faithful when nobody's looking, like enduring pain when the room is empty, like standing alone when you are misunderstood."

Reclaiming Our Lost Courage: Learning Not to Judge

We have no need to *find* courage. It is already within all of us. We simply need to reclaim it.

How can we once again become courageous? How do we find the courage to tell someone what we are really feeling? To tell them the truth? To be authentic with them? To serve them and honor others? To love them? To be truly effective in our relationships with them and in the rest of our lives? In other words, how do we find the courage to live the CASTLE Principles?

Even romantic love calls on us to be courageous, to open our hearts to another and to let them glimpse the secrets of our soul.

Sometimes, we are stretched to draw on our courage to look past our preconceptions and judgments.

Adele Azar-Rucquoi never imagined that she would find her Prince Charming among the homeless and penniless. At 59, after searching far and wide for the man of her dreams, she was close to abandoning her quest.

Then fate stepped in, as it often does—a call from her close friend Lynn changed her life forever.

"Adele, I met a man who reads Thomas Merton," she said. "His name is Jim. I want you to meet him."

Adele had passionately read everything the poet-monk ever wrote. Merton's down-to-earth pathway to God had shaped her soul, and he had said, "The biggest human temptation is to settle for too little." But there was a catch, Lynn said. Jim had no roof over his head, and had been living on the streets of Orlando for more than a year. He had no home and no money. That made him an impossible candidate for Adele, who had struggled with money issues for most of her life.

> We have what we seek, it is there all the time, and if we give it time, it will make itself known to us.
>
> *Thomas Merton*

In her youth, Adele had rebelled against her immigrant father's obsession with money, which he proudly earned through thrift and hard work, first building his own grocery store, and later acquiring Florida real estate. After graduating from college, Adele felt called to devote her life more fully to God, converting to Catholicism and escaping the issues of money by taking the vows of poverty as a nun. Sixteen years later, she left the convent and soon found herself holding down three jobs at once to meet her material needs, and it was not lost on her that she was now following the same patterns that she had earlier criticized in her father. When he passed away several years later, Adele was left with a substantial inheritance. The money she had cursed was now hers.

Now she was a wealthy woman. Why would she want to meet a homeless man, even if he did love Merton?

But her friend Lynn, who was highly intuitive and could look into a person's heart and soul without passing judgment, saw not Jim the homeless vagabond, but Jim the scholar, the poet, the philosopher—and the perfect match for Adele.

Reluctantly, Adele agreed to the breakfast meeting arranged by Lynn. Seated in the restaurant, she nervously sipped her coffee, waiting for Jim and preparing for the worst.

Don't judge a book by its cover 'til you've read the book.

Jamie Lee Curtis

Would he be in rags? Would he smell? Would he be abrasive? As she saw Lynn approaching from a distance, a tall, lanky man at her side, her fears were allayed. Jim had smoothly trimmed hair, the color of wheat, a handsome beard, and honest, blue eyes. He looked like a good-natured, absent-minded professor. Gallantly, Jim shook Adele's hand and helped the two women with their chairs. He didn't grovel or appear nervous. Instead, he chatted effortlessly about his new laptop computer. Adele marveled—a man on the street owning a laptop! It was a very strange start for a woman of means and a man of no means. Adele tried not to stare. Over bacon and eggs, she felt her composure returning.

There was no denying the attraction she felt for Jim. She was fascinated by every gesture he made and every word he spoke. What history, she wondered, lay behind those eyes and that easy smile? What had happened to this man that had caused him to fall so low? Why had he chosen this vagabond existence?

Although the conversation flowed easily, these unspoken questions created an indisputable awkwardness between them. Lynn sensed this and, as the meeting drew to a close, played match-maker again: "I hope we'll catch you at the next Merton meeting. In fact, don't worry about a way to get there—we'll pick you up," she said breezily to Jim. "That would be great," he answered, glancing at Adele.

They met twice more—first at the Merton meeting, and later at a picnic lunch to which Jim had invited her. Adele had reluctantly accepted the invitation, wondering how Jim would find the means to provide a meal. On the day of the picnic, she hesitatingly drove her car to the agreed location, but then decided to park it blocks away and walk the rest of the distance to meet Jim. The idea of pulling up in a Cadillac to greet her homeless beau seemed inappropriate.

"So, where's your car?" was the first question Jim asked. "I didn't bring it," Adele lied, lacking the courage to be truthful.

Being homeless did nothing to impair Jim's hosting skills. He served sandwiches, chips, cold drinks, and even a Mrs. Paul's cookie for dessert. He impressed Adele with his ease and resourcefulness. But their conversation soon turned to a sobering topic: Jim had chosen the occasion to openly reveal his past to Adele, answering the questions that had haunted her ever since their first meeting. Jim's story, Adele discovered, was more complex and painful than she could ever have imagined.

Deep inside, Jim's true, unrequited calling was to be an artist and a poet, but he suppressed these gifts every day, struggling to be what he was not—a success in the world of business. He had married young and found himself faced early with the need to support his wife and two children, and he therefore did what was required of him to ensure economic survival for his family. But after several years on this inauthentic path, he felt he had sunk into dark shadows, and experienced a deep sense of personal failure. His marriage fell apart.

> A man knows when he has found his vocation when he stops thinking about how to live and begins to live.
>
> *Thomas Merton*

"We broke up after 20 years," Jim told Adele, "and I headed for Key West on an extended tour of duty for the U.S. Navy Reserve. Then, after that Navy assignment, my life really took off." He shared with Adele how he had immersed himself into his writing and poetry, responding, at last, to his long repressed muse. Soon, he met and married a similarly Bohemian free spirit. But, as the days passed, Jim descended into a personal mental hell. He sought the guidance of a therapist, who advised him, "Jim, having left home, family, and everything else familiar, your stress level is off the charts."

The therapist proved right. Within a short time, Jim suffered a complete mental and emotional breakdown that led to his taking the life of his new wife. Jim was judged by three court psychiatrists to be insane at the time of his crime, and he pleaded to the lesser charge of second-degree murder. Following seven years of incarceration in Florida prisons, he was released on probation. When Lynn introduced him to Adele, Jim was living on the streets of Orlando and savoring his new freedom.

Adele sat astounded, taking in Jim's story. Although she found it extremely unsettling, she felt a calm come over her which she could only explain as grace from above. Now she knew his traumatic past—all of it. She soon realized that she would need to quickly decide whether or not she wanted to continue this relationship. She agonized over the undeniable attraction she felt for him, but ultimately concluded that there couldn't possibly be a future for her in a relationship with a homeless man who had such a troubled past.

When Jim called her to arrange another meeting, she told him, "I'm not seeing you again," immediately sensing Jim's hurt in the silence and his long sigh. Then he answered, "Okay—if that's what you want."

In the weeks that followed, Adele was haunted by thoughts of Jim and a string of synchronicities that opened a deeper awareness of him in her. She realized that it was unfair to judge him on the basis of his setbacks and tragic experiences alone, or because he had shed all his material possessions. Jim's circumstances, Adele was beginning to understand, were a spiritual passage through which he had retained his deep inner dignity, which existed independently of external conditions. She wrote him a note and sent it to the box number he had given her.

When he called her in response, he excitedly shared with her the news that he was now living with a Catholic family who attended the same church as he did—they had invited him to stay in their home in an extra bedroom. The family's trust in Jim sealed Adele's own destiny.

"Come over to Sunday-evening mass with us," Jim cheerily invited her.

A simple courtship followed, and within a couple of weeks, Adele realized that she was closer to Jim than she had ever been to any other person in her life. They were married on December 10, 1993, the anniversary of Merton's entry into the monastery at Gethsemane and his death in Bangkok 25 years later.

> The power of genuine love is so deep and so strong that it cannot be deflected from its true aim even by the silliest of wrong ideas. When love is alive and mature in a person, it does not matter if he has a false idea of himself and of life: love will guide him according to its own inner truth and will correct his ideas in spite of him.
>
> *Thomas Merton*

When we act courageously, we invite miraculous events and amazing synchronicities to enter into our lives. As Adele honored her inner courage and followed her heart by marrying Jim, she set the stage for such a miracle: Within four years, Jim discovered that he had accumulated a sizeable teacher's annuity—earned but forgotten. This, and his art, made Jim a significant contributor to the couple's finances.

The important lessons in courage—among them being brave enough to consider options beyond one's own prejudices—that Adele Azar-Rucquoi learned from meeting Jim and her eventual marriage to him, inspired her to write *Money As Sacrament: Finding the Sacred in Money* (Celestial Arts, 2002), a book for women who seek to end financial struggles and establish a peaceful relationship with money.

All these years later, their marriage is flourishing and their commitment to each other remains strong. Jim is fully engaged in life again. His self-esteem has also been nourished by successful

exhibits of his art that have won the acclaim of judges and remu-
neration from patrons.

"Growing old with Jim is pure joy," says Adele. "I made the
right choice in marrying him."

I invited Jim to write a poem for this book, and he responded:

Adele has her courage taking me on with all that baggage.
Which is my own part in this miracle of us, I wonder?
Where's the Jim once visited then abandoned by such a muse,
Spent and undeserving?
That I escaped paying with my life for the one I took,
That God, the state, then Adele conspire in this rebirth's
      hard to ignore:
Something more must be required! Love isn't finished with me.
More than ever—I must create!

Adele's courage and her deep love for Jim enabled her to look
through the facades of material possessions and past acquired
social reference points to see his authenticity. She found her
prayers for a life companion answered, but this gift could only be
gained with courage—the courage to recognize and accept the
blessing that, based on first impressions, appeared to be very
different from what she had envisaged.

Just as remarkable are the courage that both Jim and Adele
have demonstrated and the strength of their bond that has enabled
them to openly tell their story for the first time by agreeing to let
me write about it in this book. They have done so in the knowledge that in every tragic personal journey, there are lessons to be
learned and passed on, and in this case, the lessons are about being
courageous, forgiving, and loving. Their courage is an example to
us all, and sharing it so bravely inspires positive transformation in
their own lives and those of others.

Courage Has Its Rewards

Courage has its own rewards, and very often they are high. In fact, there might be a universal law at play here: "The amount of inspiration and mastery gained is directly related to the amount of courage invested."

I am a passionate skier. I ski with very good skiers because they stretch me—and sometimes they scare me. But they always love me, so I trust them. I have to gather up my courage when they urge me to ski off a 60-degree precipice, but when I have done it once and survived, and then done it again without the fear, this is one of the great joys in my life. Loving, empathetic teachers, coaches, and leaders call on us to expand our courage. When we do, we grow, and we are inspired and therefore inspire.

> The bravest thing you can do when you are not brave is to profess courage and act accordingly.
> *Corra Harris*

Courage, then, is the place where change begins. As Katharine Butler Hathaway wrote, "If you let fear of consequence prevent you from following your deepest instinct, then your life will be safe, expedient and thin." Courage is the first requirement to start a new life, enter a new relationship, inspire rather than fire an employee, lose weight, kick a habit, tell the truth, or be authentic— the next of the CASTLE Principles.

Practicing Oneness by Reclaiming Our Courage

It is so easy for us to say we should be more courageous. But it is far less easy to *be* more courageous. If this were not so, then life would be so much more straightforward. So, how can we grow our courage muscles?

- By accepting responsibility for our actions, knowing that it is up to us, not some mysterious, vague "them." Are you accepting the responsibility for being courageous? Do you hold others accountable for being courageous?

- By referencing our conscience, using it as a litmus test for what is right. Not what will get us into the least amount of trouble or be the least injury to our ego, but what is true for you in this moment. A *Fast Company* survey of readers, published on the Internet, showed that 73 percent said that responsibility and conscience are the most important conditions of courage at work, followed by love (11 percent), sacrifice (7 percent) and fear (7 percent). What is right for you now?

- By talking less about courage and acting with courage more, first with ourselves, and then with others. This will bring about a growing comfort with being courageous. Are you requiring yourself to practice the same level of courage that you expect of others?

- By remembering that courage comes from passion. If we are disengaged from life, we will have no passion for it and therefore we will be unable to draw on and use our reserves of courage. Finding the people and a cause that engage our passion will fuel our courage. When we feel intensely passionate about people, work, nature, ideas, or causes, we hardly notice the need to be courageous. In fact, there is simply no question about it: we *will* be courageous. Are you stoking the fires of your passion for life?

- By creating an environment for ourselves that is safer and therefore requires less energy to be invested in courage. Sometimes, we need courage simply because we are afraid. If we honor courage (in ourselves as well as others) we will foster the environment in which people are inspired and encouraged to be truthful and authentic. Are you inviting yourself and others to create safer environments by not being intimidating, angry, threatening, hostile, aggressive, selfish, dangerous, or political and inauthentic, so that there is less need to use courage for the inconsequential, saving it for nobler purposes?

- We get what we expect, so we get a lot of cowardice, especially in organizations. Are you rewarding acts of courage, thus inviting more of them? Do your corporate and familial codes reward courage and therefore inspire you and others to step up and be brave?

BOTTOM LINE

Why do we need Courage?

Because every important transformation begins with Courage; therefore, it is the first step towards oneness.

Reflections to Inspire Growth in Courage

Describe one of the most Courageous moments in your life—a time when you were at your personal, Courageous best:

_____

_____

_____

_____

_____

_____

Describe a current situation in your life that, in your heart, you know could be enhanced through practicing greater Courage. It is within you already, so how would you apply the same level of Courage, described in your own example above, to this current situation?

_____

_____

_____

_____

_____

_____

Do the thing you are afraid to do
and the death of fear is certain.
Ralph Waldo Emerson

6

AUTHENTICITY

THE FOUR INSTITUTIONAL bastions of our society—religion, education, politics, and business—have recently experienced a rash of problems associated with low integrity, morality, and hypocrisy. Previously, business was virtually exempt from such considerations. Few suspected that businesses would pursue the illusion of separateness to the extent of communicating untruthfully in their annual reports or stealing money. Or that business leaders would trick shareholders into buying their art collections or be jailed for fraud.

The Loss of Oneness Is the Loss of Authenticity

The high-water mark for separateness thinking in corporations was reached with Arthur Andersen, Enron, Adelphia, WorldCom, and others that followed. Even the bluest of blue-chip companies came under scrutiny for their business practices. People want to know whether organizations made their numbers legitimately or did so by buying back stock or withdrawing

> The first step is to penetrate the clouds of deceit and distortion and learn the truth about the world, then to organize and act to change it. That's never been impossible and never been easy.
> *Noam Chomsky*

deposits from employees' pension funds or capitalizing expenses or engineering bankruptcy in order to avoid liabilities.

There are genuine concerns about the viability of what were once thought of as pillars of business and society—the kind of companies whose shares we recommended to our mothers.

Consider General Motors and the challenges it faces. Only 160,000 employees still work at GM in the United States, even though there are more than a million retirees and their families who rely on the firm for a security blanket through pension payments. The annual cost of the health-care portion alone is $6 billion, costing GM more than it spends on steel each year. Medical expenses for GM's more than one million employees, retirees, and dependants now account for $1,500 of the price of every car and truck it sells, and that amount is increasing by at least 10 percent a year. It is clear that this cannot be sustained— GM is undergoing wrenching layoffs and union concessions in order to right its money-losing business.

GM is probably no less secure than many organizations, but this is faint praise, underscoring the widespread nature of the risks and the growing need for transparency and authenticity in working life. People's futures depend on it. It will take courage for GM to develop the authentic relationships necessary to work out solutions that meet the needs of all parties. True authenticity may help avert the largest bankruptcy of an industrial company in history.

How did we arrive at this critical point? Evidently the pressure to perform has caused businesses to take risks of integrity and prudence that have compromised their authenticity and principles and therefore their future.

Arthur Andersen was the accounting firm of the public company I ran. When I was asked to personally negotiate a very subtle and substantial financial payment to governments in the Middle East— because that's the way business is done there—Arthur Andersen advised me not to do it.

"This is against the law," they told me. "You're being asked to do this in ways that are not legal. Doing business this way is contrary to the provisions of the Foreign Corrupt Practices Act in the U.S."

The firm provided an effective second opinion for our own conscience.

But Arthur Andersen does not exist in its original form anymore. It failed because it moved away from its own standards. In October 2001, Texas-based Enron, which was Andersen's largest client, was subjected to federal investigation after admitting to massive bookkeeping fraud. Lawyers for Andersen immediately and vigorously began to remind Andersen employees to shred documents in line with company policy. Over the next four weeks, the company engaged in what the government called an "unprecedented campaign of document destruction," shredding two tons of paperwork. They stopped the practice only when faced with a government subpoena.[8]

The Justice Department accused Andersen of trying to obscure the firm's role in hiding Enron's fraud. Andersen responded that it was simply following a long-standing policy on destroying notes and draft documentation. A Houston jury disagreed and convicted Andersen of obstruction of justice, for which they received the maximum sentence of a $500,000 fine and five years' probation.

Under the weight of the indictment and conviction, Andersen collapsed, shrinking its U.S. workforce from 28,000 to 200 people, most of whom were there just to handle matters relating to shareholder litigation. Although the decision was later overturned by the U.S. Supreme Court, the damage had been done.

Andersen had been advising its customers inadequately, to the point that confidence in the firm had evaporated. What they said and what they did were out of alignment. If an accounting firm—or any firm for that matter—does not have the confidence of its

---

8. Jan Crawford Greenburg, *Chicago Tribune*, June 1, 2005

clients, it can't continue to exist. And that's what happened. In the same way that lack of confidence can cause a run on a bank, Andersen clients, doubting the firm's authenticity, began leaving in droves. The loss of business was so drastic, the firm imploded.

Arthur Andersen was challenged and eventually destroyed because its partners became greedy and inauthentic. They became that way because they viewed themselves as separate from their customers and community, instead of realizing they were all one.

In a conspiracy of inauthenticity, Andersen went along with what its client Enron wanted to do—the opposite of what its response would have been years earlier. It is easy to see how things can go awry. Andersen knew that to refuse Enron's actions would cause them to lose the mega corporation's business. They couldn't afford to lose Enron, and so they compromised their principles by issuing incorrect financial statements, failing to inform the board of directors or the Audit and Compliance Committee, and shredding incriminating evidence.

> The most exhausting thing in life, I have discovered, is insincerity.
> *Anne Morrow Lindbergh*

Tyco International's former chairman, Dennis Kozlowski, and former finance chief, Mark Swartz, were accused of secretly forgiving loans to themselves, claiming undeserved bonuses, and undertaking fraudulent stock sales to bolster their wealth. Tyco, which owns ADT, the largest security firm in the world, is a fundamentally strong company of high-quality products, but these men's actions put it under a cloud of greed. When Ed Breen was drafted as CEO to clean up the mess after Kozlowski's ouster, his commitment to authenticity was total. The arrival of a courageous and authentic leader has enabled the organization to regain its vitality.

This experience of flawed corporate leadership is duplicated in the accusations that we have seen tossed at members of the priesthood in the Catholic Church. It is seen in the school system, both in North America and elsewhere in the world.

What is happening is that the custodians of the message, upon whom we used to rely as keepers of the truth, are practicing something different from what they preach—a lack of authenticity.

Why We Need Authenticity

As we discussed in the previous chapter, the first step toward becoming authentic is to be courageous. Authenticity is not possible without courage, because authenticity is about being real. If we don't have courage, we cannot be real. It is not until we reclaim the necessary courage that we can become real. And being real, in turn, requires us to be brave enough to reveal, own, and often share our truth, our fears, our emotions, and our vulnerabilities. This is how we become authentic. Authenticity, then, is the next step upon which we need to focus in our quest to become one—the key to engagement in life.

The most terrifying thing is to accept oneself completely.
Carl Jung

We need to be authentic because we love how authentic people touch our hearts and inspire us.

An elderly woman and her little grandson, whose face was sprinkled with bright freckles, spent the day at the zoo. They joined a lineup of children waiting to get their cheeks painted by a local artist, who was decorating them with tiger paws.

"You've got so many freckles, there's no place to paint!" said a girl in the line to the boy.

The little boy dropped his head. His grandmother knelt down next to him.

"I love your freckles," she said, tracing her finger across the child's cheek. "When I was a little girl, I always wanted freckles. Freckles are beautiful."

The boy looked up. "Really?" he said.

Of course," replied the grandmother. "Why, just name me one thing that's prettier than freckles."

The little boy thought for a moment, peered into his grand-mother's face and whispered, "Wrinkles."

Authenticity: Oneness of Thought, Word, Feeling, and Deed

Seeing someone else displaying compassion, love, and grace gives our hearts permission to open, and we embrace that authentic person for their courage. This is the practice of the conscious leader. Authenticity, as much as anything, generates love in the hearts of others because it fills such a deep human need. Our souls cry out for authenticity. With it, we can build relationships and inspire one another and our communities, families, friends, customers, colleagues, and suppliers. The opportunities for increased revenues are obvious. What a gift—a "technique" for both nourishing the soul and inspiring the personality.

What is authenticity?

When we are authentic, our minds, mouths, hearts, and our feet are one. We think, say, feel, and do the same thing in complete alignment. This is how we become real: by ensuring that what our minds think, what our hearts feel, what our mouths speak, and where our feet walk are one and the same. As we learned from Machiavelli, we will remain inauthentic as long as we practice separateness between what we think, say, feel, and do.

Being authentic sometimes requires us to be humble, to reveal our foibles or imperfections.

A mother brought her son to Gandhi, explaining to him that he ate too much sugar, and she asked Gandhi to convince her son to stop. She had tried herself, but thought the message might be more effectively delivered by Gandhi. Gandhi, known as Mahatma (great soul), asked the mother to return with her son in a week.

When mother and son returned, Gandhi asked the son to stop eating sugar, and the child agreed. Observing this, the mother said to Gandhi, "My child has agreed to what you asked. Why could you not have given him the same advice the first time I came?"

"Madam," said Gandhi, "a week ago, I was still eating sugar."

Authenticity, then, is complete oneness in our thinking, speaking, feeling, and doing. It is head, mouth, heart, and feet all communicating and living the same message. This means that we consciously think, say, feel, and do the same thing in all aspects of our lives—as leaders, of course, but also as parents, children, friends, and spouses. *Any* relationship is enhanced, and often made whole, through authenticity. Indeed, it is the alignment of all these aspects that enables us to experience this longed-for sense of oneness.

> Happiness is when what you think, what you say, and what you do are in harmony.
> *Mohandas Gandhi*

The Whitewater Rule

One of my passions is whitewater—canoeing, kayaking, rafting; few things are as exhilarating as being one with nature's energy in a river, moving through whitewater. Even the stillness of a calm river or a serene lake is deeply nourishing to my soul—a meditation and connection with the essence of the Earth.

If you study whitewater enthusiasts, especially those with great skills, you'll notice that they never argue with the water. One of the earliest lessons whitewater novices discover is that there is no gain in opposing the natural forces of the water—the rapids have far greater power than most humans can muster. Mastery of whitewater skills does not mean "mastering" the rapids—they cannot be overwhelmed by force or controlled. Instead, whitewater experts learn how to *read* the authenticity of the water—interpreting the innate energy of the rapids—and then they learn how to ride the power of the water, using the muscles of the rapids to be carried safely forwards. I think of following the energy as the *Whitewater Rule.* I have sometimes paddled to an eddy just downstream from

Nothing in the world is
softer and weaker
than water;

But for attacking the hard
and strong, there is
nothing like it!

For nothing can take
its place.

That the weak overcomes
the strong, and the soft
overcomes the hard,

This is something
known by all, but
practiced by none.

Lao-Tzu

a large rock in the river and positioned my craft precisely in the current. This is known as "surfing"—the water is stable in this unique place, flowing gently in the opposite direction to the rest of the river. Here, one can relax indefinitely pointing upstream, while the rapids roar by on both sides. This is a metaphor for life. Whitewater is a permanent condition for most of us. We can attempt the futile: trying to overwhelm the energy; or we can harness and ride it: flowing with the energy—the *Whitewater Rule*. Following the energy requires less effort and engages the powerful forces that are moving in the direction in which you wish to travel anyway.

One of my favorite places for canoeing is Algonquin Park, nearly 8,000 square kilometers (3,000 square miles) of pristine wilderness in Ontario, Canada. There, one summer, I reflected on my experience with whitewater:

Zen River

Steal away, my sons and daughters,
To the mountain streams and lakes,
To the land of rapid waters,
Where I learned about mistakes.

Gently launching, guide your craft out,
Paddle bravely from the shore.
Feel the sense of growing self-doubt
Weaken faith you had before.

Rushing waters grin and grasp you,
Steal your courage with a jeer.
Stretch and strain with every sinew,
Pitting power over fear.

Wrestle vainly with those rapids –
They will fight and cost you dear,
While her secret to your ear bids
If you're wise enough to hear.

Mighty River knows the wise way –
Just surrender to the flow,
As she whispers to you gently,
"I'm your friend and not your foe."

Life is a river, smooth and tough,
Plenty of power to spare.
She gives you a choice: play with her rough,
Or seize her offer to share.

Authenticity is like the whitewater: read the original, authentic source of power, recognize it, and ride it. When we try to fight it—as in life, when we try to fight our inner truths, our authenticity—it simply becomes an obstacle course, and eventually it will undo us and spill us into the turbulence.

The rule for life is to follow the energy—this enables us to become authentic.

We all yearn for authentic leaders who can be trusted to do as they say, who flow with the natural energy of their inner truths. Authentic leaders have an air of transparency about them. And followers want conscious leaders who are clear about what they stand for, what their values are, and who live these values consistently.

Authenticity Comes from a Loving Heart

A friend of mine, who knew Mother Teresa well, explained to me that everyone associated with her had no doubt about what she stood for. It was just the way she showed up. That's how she lived her life, gave her gifts, and contributed her energy to this world. All her actions and communications arose directly from her authenticity.

Mother Teresa once visited an elderly aboriginal man who lived on an Australian reservation in great poverty and destitution—one of the most difficult situations she had ever seen. He had no friends, no visitors, and his home was a slovenly mess.

"Please, let me clean your house, wash your clothes, and make your bed," Mother Teresa said, to which the elderly man responded, "I'm okay like this. Let it be."

"You will be still better if you allow me to do it," she said.

He finally agreed. While she was cleaning his house and washing his clothes, she discovered a beautiful lamp that was covered with dust. It had not been lit for many years.

"Don't you light your lamp?" she asked. "Don't you ever use it?"

"No. No one comes to see me. I have no need to light it. Who would I light it for?"

Mother Teresa asked him if he would light it daily for the Sisters if they visited every night.

"Of course," he replied.

The Sisters began to visit him every evening, and each day they cleaned the lamp and lit it.

Two years later, having forgotten about this incident, Mother Teresa received a letter from the elderly man. "Tell my friend that the light she lit in my life continues to shine still," the message said.

The loving heart is the source of inspiration. Mother Teresa's authenticity originated in the clear sense of purpose she had for her life. She knew why she was on Earth, what she stood for, and what she wanted to do—her destiny, cause, and calling.[9] This made her an authentic leader—someone who is inspired and who inspires others. It was her authenticity that caused her to be loved by so many.

Everyone hopes that what they see is what they'll get from others. We always hope that others will not play low-integrity games with us, that they will not say one thing when they are actually thinking something else. We can easily accept that they are conflicted, or confused, or perhaps not even ready yet to make a decision, but we all hope that they will be authentic about their position, even when it is unclear.

Never say 'Hello' if you really mean 'Goodbye.'

Never say you want something if you're never willing to try.

Never say you're going to if you never plan to start.

Never hold my hand if you know you'll break my heart.

Anonymous

Being authentic does not mean that there won't be situations where our hearts and minds don't agree. I can remain authentic by being very clear and honest about how I feel right now, even if I'm feeling ambivalent. I can say to you, "I don't know yet where I stand on this, because how I feel about it is not the same as how I *think* about it. But what you can be sure of is that when I am ready, what I *say* I will do, will be the same thing as what I will *actually* do." This is the statement of an authentic person who has chosen to practice the principles of oneness.

Nor does being authentic prevent us from changing our minds. This is everyone's prerogative. We all listen, learn, grow, and evolve, and this can result in our seeing things differently over time. But we can still retain our authenticity throughout this process, explaining to others that our learning has caused us to change our opinion.

---

9. For detailed information about the concept of "Destiny, Cause, and Calling," please see my book *Inspire! What Great Leaders Do* (John Wiley & Sons, 2004), and also http://www.secretan.com/inspire.

Authenticity Is the Root of Trust

On the other hand, it is the deliberate lack of authenticity in a leader that is so especially resented by followers. If I tell you, "I will vote for this proposition at the next board meeting," and then vote differently when that day comes, I am being inauthentic. My words and my deeds are not one. Yet this is the behavior that too frequently characterizes modern organizations at many levels. When the thoughts, words, feelings, and deeds of those we trust become separated, we lose faith, and ask, "Why would I believe you or listen to you if what you say and what you do are different?" The loss we experience is the loss of authenticity, which leads to a loss of trust.

We yearn to trust people. Friendships, marriages, family relationships, teams, customer and vendor relationships, and international relations all depend on trust. And trust is the result of consistency. We trust those whom, over time, we have observed to be consistent in the oneness of what they think, say, feel, and do. It is the consistency of repeated authenticity that forms the basis of our relationship, which is built on trust.

Authentic Leadership versus Spin

Our bookstores overflow with tomes on leadership written by corporate leaders. These carefully reconstructed, veneered, and varnished versions of their accomplishments are high on financial performance and marketing. Their writers spin many yarns of personal triumph and brilliance. But readers often sense inauthenticity. The stories of these leaders have sometimes been airbrushed more than the photos of aging actors. There are no admissions of vulnerability or miscalculation. There is scant mention of these leaders' routines of firing the bottom-performing 10 percent of every department year after year. Nothing is said about the ruthless drive of their companies for market penetration and domination, and the shuttering of departments or divisions that do not reach the number one or two position in their categories in the marketplace.

Often, there are greater lessons from observing the lives of people who *live fully* in their authenticity, warts and all. Bono, for example, perhaps the world's best-known rock star, does more to eliminate AIDS in Africa, and to cancel third-world debt, than any other human being on the planet. He connects with world leaders and courageously and authentically tweaks their consciences, urging them to become more engaged and sympathetic to the problems of third-world countries. Authentic leadership is also well represented by Sting, another musical icon. He has done so much for indigenous peoples in South America and for Amnesty International. These are inspiring leaders who wear their courage and authenticity openly, living them every day for all to see. Thus, they are models of the gritty reality of authenticity. We want to know, How does this work for them? Why are they doing it? As leaders, what is there for us to learn from their lives that might be useful to ours, about genuineness and authenticity?

> If being an egomaniac means that I believe in what I do and in my art or my music, then in that respect you can call me that. I believe in what I do, and I'll say it.
>
> *John Lennon*

Courage, as I suggested in the previous chapter, is not about telling someone else to be courageous, but about becoming courageous oneself. Similarly, authenticity in a leader, like all of the CASTLE Principles, in fact, is not about telling someone else to be authentic—it is about how we each behave, and therefore model, being authentic ourselves. In our company, we have an expression, "What are you teaching when you are not speaking?" Great teaching, like great leadership, comes from the authenticity of the teacher.

The practice of oneness in aligning our thoughts, words, feelings, and deeds is a very personal affair. It has more to do with *me* and how I live and behave, than with my desire to fix *others*. It is about how I show up, not about how *they* should do so. It is about how we each choose to connect to our inner values and live them.

Inauthentic behavior can manifest in many different and strange ways. Consider how in May 2004, 38,000 illegal copies of the film *The Passion of the Christ* were downloaded from the Internet. *Business Week* writers were moved to observe, "So much for 'thou shalt not steal.'"[10]

So, we turn away from the superficial examples and search in different places for reliable partners, friends, customers, employees, suppliers, teachers, coaches, and leaders. All of us need and yearn for others who can guide us, who can be the light on our path and help us restore the trust we have lost in organizations, churches, families, or nations. Such people restore our sense of personal oneness with them because what they think, say, feel, and do are the same thing.

The Power of Authenticity to Earn Trust

Inspiring people in this new and different business and social environment depends on a new level of transparency and authenticity. This is how conscious leaders are earning back the confidence of employees, shareholders, and customers. In some cases, this may take a long time and much effort.

When the *Exxon Valdez* oil spill occurred in 1989, many people boycotted Exxon products, and millions still do, angered that the company has refused to pay the $4.5 billion in court-ordered punitive damages to the thousands of fishing workers who were bankrupted or forced out of business. For some, it may be

---

10. *Business Week*, June 28, 2004, p. 14

20 years before they forgive Exxon. And that's the way customers behave. They are connected in so many ways—there is no separation. If customers don't like a company's standards, or ethics, or what a company stands for, they'll withdraw their purchasing dollars. And if ten million other people feel the same way, that organization may experience a formidable challenge.

The reverse is just as true. Many people make a conscious effort to purchase products and services from companies whose policies and ethics are strong and transparent and reflect authenticity. People go out of their way to fly Southwest Airlines, for instance, because they know that they're a great company. People may know nothing about the technology of their airplanes, air-traffic control, or baggage handling, but they know they have 800 married couples working for them, that they put employees' interests above *everything* else, including those of customers and share-holders, and that their teamwork leads to operating costs that are lower than those of many others in the industry. All of that tells potential customers a great deal about the authenticity of their corporate culture and causes them to choose to support them and give them their business whenever they can.

This is not so much based on science as it is based on myth, mystery, and magic. It is an example of operating from a philosophy of oneness instead of separation. Southwest knows that treating people well creates an awareness in the community that translates into lower costs (half the industry average) and increased revenues (a market capitalization equal to three times the rest of the airline industry combined).

The Wegmans supermarket chain, based in Rochester, New York, has been rated the best company to work for in America by *Fortune* magazine. When its chairman, Robert Wegman, was asked why he lavished extensive benefits on employees, he remarked, with an obvious reference to oneness, "I was no different from them." Like Southwest Airlines, Starbucks, FedEx, Pella, Medtronics, Alaska

Wildland Adventures (see chapter 7), and Men's Wearhouse (see chapter 10), Wegmans values employees just as highly as customers— quite contrary to the usual corporate mantra of separation, which puts "customers first." This is not only unusual; it is magical—and owes very little to separateness and everything to oneness.

Treat people with deep authenticity and honor their spirits as Wegmans does, and you will become *the* grocery chain to work for and to shop at, with margins twice those of the big four grocers, sales per square foot 50 percent greater than the industry average, a staff turnover of 6 percent compared to 19 percent for the industry, and 7,000 people who write each year pleading with you to open a store in their neighborhood.

Wegmans has given $54 million in scholarships to more than 17,500 full- and part-time employees over the past 20 years. Says Wegman, "I have never given away more than I got back."

This is pure authentic engagement with employees. Says Sara Goggins, college student and part-time grocery clerk, "I love this place. If teaching doesn't work out, I would so totally work at Wegmans."

Similarly, authenticity attracts people to the Body Shop, where they buy a bath oil or lip balm not just because they like the product, but also because they know the company stands for fairness, justice, fair trade, and the environment. This stand is evidenced especially through its support of Amnesty International and the indigenous peoples of South America. The Body Shop is truly transparent about its values. It champions women's rights and freedoms and social justice and campaigns against domestic violence. This is what the company is best known for—its raw, no-excuses authenticity, which is expressed in such practices as sourcing products directly from indigenous peoples instead of through middle men, and paying them fairly. The Body Shop has never spent a penny on advertising, allowing its reputation for authenticity to carry its brand. When customers shop there, they are making a statement: they are supporting the authenticity of the Body Shop.

Not only do people like to buy from authentic companies, they also like to work for them. Southwest Airlines receives more than 150,000 applications each year for around 5,000 job openings.

Organizations that practice authenticity are very public in their declarations, transparently partnering with the public, and inviting feedback that strengthens their authenticity. Starbucks uses six "Guiding Principles" to measure the appropriateness of their decisions—authenticity worn unapologetically for all to see. These are:

1. Provide a great work environment and treat each other with respect and dignity.
2. Embrace diversity as an essential component in the way we do business.
3. Apply the highest standards of excellence to the purchasing, roasting and fresh delivery of our coffee.
4. Develop enthusiastically satisfied customers all of the time.
5. Contribute positively to our communities and our environment.
6. Recognize that profitability is essential to our future success.

Authenticity—displayed through a combination of gritty reality (commitment to profit and excellence) and oneness (commitment to respect, dignity, diversity, enthusiasm, satisfaction, community, and the environment). This openness and commitment to people and the environment has a way of engaging people—especially customers—in ways that marketing experts consistently misread. Case studies on Starbucks are widely taught, but the "secret" of Starbucks' success is usually attributed to their savvy marketing and seldom to their authentic commitment to creating a business that connects to the soul. Such a conclusion would seem way too "touch-feely" for many—yet this is the level of authenticity that people yearn for and are willing to support by paying a fair price for products purchased from an authentic company. As Colleen Barrett, Southwest's president, puts it, "Others can copy our business plan, but they can't copy our People" (she always spells "people" with a capital "P"!).

Authenticity on Wall Street

In 2004, Time Warner sold its music division, Warner Music, the third largest music company in the U.S., to Edgar Bronfman Jr. and a group of private equity firms led by Thomas H. Lee Partners. Early in 2005, Warner called several big Wall Street firms to arrange to sell its shares to the public in an initial public offering (IPO). Warner Music chose two banks to lead the IPO, who in turn invited others to support them. Merrill Lynch, among others, jumped at the opportunity to participate in such a lucrative deal—after all, each underwriter stood to share in a pool of $26.3 million. And it was in Warner Music's best interests for Merrill Lynch to be involved because the top media analyst at Merrill Lynch, Jessica Reif Cohen, was, according to the *Hollywood Reporter*, one of the 100 most powerful women in show business. Reif Cohen's endorsement would count a great deal with investors.

Merrill Lynch told Warner Music that they thought they could sell the shares to the public at around $30 each.

Two years earlier, the Securities and Exchange Commission had approved a settlement of civil claims against ten of Wall Street's largest firms in a historic $1.4-billion deal that brought an end to several probes into alleged conflicts of interest that had hurt investors. Following these settlements, new procedures were adopted for valuing IPOs. Research analysts were now required to make assessments of a client's business prospects independently of the opinions of the underwriters.

Warner Music summoned Jessica Reif Cohen and the analysts from all the other underwriting banks for a briefing at its headquarters in the Rockefeller Center. After the PowerPoint presentations, the comparisons to EMI and other music giants, and reviews of the expanding digital music market, Reif Cohen spent two weeks writing her report. Her verdict was that a $25 or $30 issue price (suggested by Warner and the bankers) was unrealistic and that $17 would be closer to the mark. A Merrill Lynch banker described the impact of this assessment as "a nightmare."

"What were we supposed to do?" he said. "We couldn't sell the deal to investors if Jessica was going to be telling everyone our client was worthless."

Before the earlier Wall Street settlement, a bold move of opposing a firm's investment bankers would have cost an analyst like Reif Cohen their job unless they bowed under pressure and withdrew their dissenting opinion. But Merrill Lynch chose the path of authenticity, deciding to abandon the offering despite the steep price of losing a highly prestigious client and several million dollars in fees. Their withdrawal from the offering sent a signal to Warner Music and all of the other bankers, causing them to lower their targets for raising money from investors. In the end, the actual price at which the shares were sold—$17, just as Reif Cohen had predicted—valued the company at nearly $1 billion less than Warner had hoped, saving investors millions.

Which bank would you like to do business with? One that ignores the valuations of its internal analysts because it could cost the firm millions of dollars in lost commissions to do so? Or one that authentically changes direction in the best interests of customers, thus raising its reputation for integrity? Authenticity like this may be costly in the short term, but is enormously beneficial in the long term.

This little-known development is a very encouraging signal of positive change. Authenticity on Wall Street has been in limited supply for years, and similar examples of authentic behavior will serve to inspire investor confidence in the future. If integrity takes up permanent residence on Wall Street, it will be because of the

Why are we surprised when fig trees bear figs?
Margaret Titzel

bold and compelling acts of integrity and authenticity taken by people and companies like Reif Cohen and her employer, Merrill Lynch. It will be because companies understand that issuer, customer, client, banker, and regulator are all one—a single, interdependent market where authenticity and integrity are the real and most valuable currency.

Practicing Oneness by Reclaiming Our Authenticity

There are some simple steps to reclaiming oneness through becoming authentic again.

- Ask yourself, "Is it true?" In a CFO Magazine survey of senior finance executives, 24 percent said that not contributing cash to their company's political action committee could be detrimental to their jobs. Another 16 percent were not sure. There is likely as much speculation as fact in these data—they are often not true because sometimes, when we are inauthentic, we simply make things up. Then, based on this fiction, we indulge in separateness thinking, pursuing policies that are out of alignment with our personal values. Check in with your mind and heart: Do you project your beliefs onto people or situations?
- Are you listening to your own inner voice? Authenticity means listening to your conscience, and acting on it, even when many voices around you are offering conflicting guidance. Becoming authentic is another step in ending the practice of trading wholeness for approval. This is how we become whole again and one with each other.

- Have you removed your personal filters and shields in order to listen authentically?
- Have you checked in with your head, mouth, heart, and feet by asking yourself, "Are what I am thinking, saying, feeling, and doing aligned as one?"
- Are you practicing the necessary courage to act authentically, pursuing what is true for you, according to your inner alignment, so that you can become one?
- Do you enjoy a reputation for authenticity?

BOTTOM LINE

Why do we need Authenticity?
Because internal alignment—oneness—is spiritually,
emotionally, and physically healing, builds relationships,
and helps us to become one, first within ourselves,
and then with others.

REFLECTIONS TO INSPIRE GROWTH IN AUTHENTICITY

Describe one of the most Authentic moments in your life, when you were at your personal, Authentic best:

_____

_____

_____

_____

_____

Describe a current situation in your life that, in your heart, you know could be enhanced through practicing greater Courage. It is within you already, so how would you apply the same level of Courage, described in your own example above, to this current situation?

_____

_____

_____

_____

_____

And if we are to be any better,
now is the time to begin.
Alfred Tennyson

7

CASTLE

SERVICE

SERVICE IS THE PURPOSE of life. We exist in order to make the world at least a little better than we found it. Our lives relate to the world in terms of how well we serve, and the legacy of each one of us will be measured accordingly. When we serve others, we become one with them.

Leadership of organizations—and families or churches or governments—is not just about those at the top. Instead, it is a delicate interplay of the dynamic between the leader and the followers, and particularly the quality of that dynamic, that determines organizational success. Frequently, the quality of the dynamic between leaders and followers, parents and children, clergy and parishioners, or politicians and constituents is determined by how well they serve each other and by how well, together, they serve the larger community—how well we respect the oneness of the whole.

> Success has nothing to do with what you gain in life or accomplish for yourself. It's what you do for others.
> *Danny Thomas*

Servant-Leadership Is Non-Competitive

Competition is the opposite of service.

Like all of the CASTLE Principles, service is a very simple concept to understand, even if it is difficult to practice. Service is about listening to others and meeting their needs with a loving heart. Conscious leaders know that the primary purpose of leadership is to serve the needs of followers. If this were not so, why would we need a leader? Followers are the customers of the leader. But this is a difficult concept for many leaders to practice, because they are often stuck in an old-story paradigm that suggests the main purpose of followers (employees) is to serve "the boss."

> Service is the rent we pay to be living. It is the very purpose of life and not something you do in your spare time.
>
> *Marian Wright Edelman*

Conscious leaders are servant-leaders who serve their followers by inviting feedback and advice from them about how they would best like to be served. This is no different from the process we use with customers in our markets, except that this is an internal rather than an external market. Whether it is through listening, compassion, caring, coaching, intuition, or vision, the conscious leader provides support to followers to enable them to realize *their* full potential.

The self-serving nature of unconscious leaders—their commitment to their ego or ambitions—is what followers greatly resent, because it reflects the pursuit of ruthless competitiveness and aggression.

Competition drives many aspects of our society, including its very youngest members. There are countless books on how to make your baby smarter and more intelligent than the next baby, even before birth. Competitiveness is drilled into our children in daycare, kindergarten, and elementary school.

Competition expresses itself in its ugliest form when it is ruthless and adversarial, a style with which our culture has become deeply saturated and to which we are now dangerously addicted. Ruthless, adversarial sports are those in which the point of the contest is to overwhelm or diminish an opponent, often described as an "enemy" to be "defeated," and frequently involving physical violence.

We introduce our children to ruthless, adversarial sports at very young and vulnerable ages, urging upon them the importance of winning. Parents even engage in fights with each other or with coaches to secure their children's winning status. The National Hockey League, perennially distracted by aggressive contests between the NHL Players' Association and the NHL owners, routinely struggles to contain ever-present and escalating parental violence. Children learn their behaviors directly from their parents—for better or worse.

A sport when practiced with gallantry, elegance, and grace, on the other hand, is more aligned with the original Olympic ideals of excellence and personal mastery. The intention of Baron Pierre de Coubertin, when he founded the modern Olympic Games (they are "games," not "competitions"), was to create an international showcase for the spirits, minds, and bodies of athletes endeavoring to excel and achieve higher standards than those presently existing, thus fulfilling the Olympic motto.

This motto came about through a friend of the Baron, Father Henri Martin Didon, of the Dominican order, who was principal of the Arcueil College near Paris. A dynamic teacher, he used the discipline of sport as a powerful character-building and educational tool. One day, following an inter-schools athletics meeting, Father Didon ended his speech with brilliant oratorical flair, quoting three words, "Citius, Altius, Fortius" (faster, higher, stronger). Struck by the succinctness of this phrase, Baron Pierre de Coubertin made it the Olympic motto, pointing out that "athletes need *freedom of excess*. That is why we gave them this motto...a motto for people who dare to try to break records."

The ideal of sports played at this noble level, compared to modern ruthless, adversarial sports, is reflected in the Olympic

Creed, which Pierre de Coubertin was inspired to write after hearing a speech given by Bishop Ethelbert Talbot at a service for Olympic champions during the 1908 Olympic Games. In part, the Olympic Creed reads:

> *The most important thing in the Olympic Games is not to win but to take part, just as the most important thing in life is not the triumph but the struggle.*

Even the Olympic flag stands for the principles of oneness. Created by Pierre de Coubertin in 1914, the Olympic flag depicts five interconnected rings on a white background. The five rings symbolize the five significant continents and are interconnected to symbolize the *friendship* (not ruthless, adversarial competition) inherent in these international games. The rings, from left to right, are blue, yellow, black, green, and red. These colors were chosen because at least one of them appeared on the flag of every country in the world—a visual tribute to our oneness.

How far from these hopes and ideals much of modern ruthless, adversarial sports have drifted! The unconscious leader who still views the world through a lens of separateness uses ruthless, adversarial sports as a metaphor for war, which is the ultimate expression of separateness and the antithesis of oneness.

On October 7, 2001, the Sunday when the United States and Great Britain began to bomb Afghanistan, video images of the attack were flashed across the stadium scoreboard at Lowe's Motor Speedway in Concord, North Carolina, as race cars zoomed around the track below. Like ancient Romans cheering their favorite gladiators, the crowd roared its approval. Meanwhile, over in Atlanta's Georgia Dome, a public-address announcer interrupted the first quarter of the Falcons–Bears game to announce the attacks. Football fans rose, applauded, and chanted, "U-S-A! U-S-A!" just as they might have cheered for their team. The boundaries between ruthless, adversarial sports and war have become merged—they are now interchangeable.

President Eisenhower once made the famous declaration that "the true mission of American sports is to prepare young people for war." *Boston Globe* columnist Jan Freeman has supported this widely held perspective by writing that sports were "invented precisely to serve as ritualized battles," both making the battlefield language inevitable and giving it a deemed legitimacy. Researchers have shown that competition makes people more aggressive and that there is a positive correlation between cultures that are warlike and those that encourage ruthless adversarial sports. None of this is inspiring to people whose major life interests lie outside of stadiums or war zones. We yearn for savvy, brilliant, yet non-aggressive, caring, serving leaders—and athletes—the kind Woodrow Wilson had in mind when he said, "You are here to enable the world to live more amply, with greater vision, and with a finer spirit of hope and achievement. You are here to enrich the world."

Many people lack a strong internal identity and therefore seek a surrogate identity outside of themselves. Thus, their personal identity can often be so wrapped up in ruthless, adversarial sports and the need for "their side" to win, that they live their lives vicariously—and separately from themselves—through the crushing performance of their favorite team. Quite often, in our intensive leadership retreats, participants ask us to provide some time out (to use a sporting term) so they can watch a particular game. Sometimes, when participants arrive on the following morning, they appear upset and depressed, and when we ask them why, they answer: "My team lost!" For many people, their team's loss can be such a shock to the ego that it causes them to become dispirited and to see the world and their entire life through a lens of despair.

It's as if we were tapping into the very worst excesses of the Roman Empire, where violent energies were unleashed in vicious fighting among gladiators. This thirst for blood is aggressively fed today in sports and media. In hockey, for example, the more violent the game, the better it is considered to be. And American children, who watch an average of four hours of TV a day, will have witnessed 12,000 murders and more than 150,000 other acts of violence by the time they finish elementary school. The National Television Violence Study in 1995 found that in 73 percent of all violent scenes, the perpetrator went unpunished. We encourage and condone violence and separateness. It is not surprising, then, that this is the style that commonly shows up in leadership practice.

Yet we are not born bloodthirsty. In fact, our brains are not even hardwired at birth to think in competitive terms. According to Joseph Chilton Pearce, author of *The Biology of Transcendence: A Blueprint of the Human Spirit* (Park Street Press, 2004), a major growth spurt of the brain occurs in the days and weeks following birth, and this process is influenced by the mother's emotional state, as well as by the stimulation and interactions provided by the mother and other caregivers. The way the brain is used, based on what is being modeled, is how it forms and grows and facilitates impulses from the sensory and emotional systems. The infant's caregivers, therefore, bear the primary responsibility for helping shape the child's reasoning and thought processes during this critical period—defining whether the child will more readily embrace separateness or oneness.

Perhaps we may hope for a new era in thinking about competition versus service. "In the wake of the terrorist attacks," wrote *USA Today*'s Christine Brennan, "our hyperbolic, self-serving and often militaristic vernacular must change." The *Rocky Mountain News* pledged, "We shall never again refer to a long touchdown pass as a bomb."

> It matters not whether you win or lose; what matters is whether I win or lose.
>
> *Darrin Weinberg*

A competitive, ruthless, adversarial, win-lose philosophy is a philosophy of separation: "Your loss is my gain." There is no sense of wholeness or being one with a larger universe in this approach. This is the toxic soil in which wars, poverty, greed, violence, and corporate despair and chronic underperformance thrive.

Servant-leaders know that life is not a blood sport, that it is not about aggression, violence, and ruthless, adversarial competition, nor about making someone else lose or feel separate. Servant-leadership offers a completely different mindset: a shift from the outmoded and separatist win-lose notion to the inclusive idea that we all have the option to help everyone win, with winning defined as, "Going as far as you can using everything that you have got." The point is oneness.

The greatest servant-leaders in history—Christ, Buddha, Confucius, and Gandhi among them—would never have supported, or even been a part of, the violence and aggression portrayed in our media. Such modes of behavior and expression would have been in total opposition to their beliefs and the way they lived their lives—committed to oneness.

The Choice: To Wound or to Serve

A non-serving relationship leads to a competitive relationship, in which I'm trying to beat you, or you're trying to trick me. This is separateness. It is not inspiring to either party. What is inspiring to followers or customers is a leader who serves, because they know that you and they are one, and their purpose is to make the combination whole.

> Only a life lived for others is a life worthwhile.
> *Albert Einstein*

In our relations with others, we have two choices. We can be aggressive, competitive, dominating, and wounding, all of which use negative, separating energy. Or we can serve, out of positive, inclusive energy that leads to oneness. We can invest our energy—and therefore lose it—in defeating someone else, making them separate. Or we can invest it in serving them and thus enhancing the sum of us both, because we are one. The ruthless, adversarial, competitive energy destroys; the inclusive energy builds, heals, and leads to a sense of personal wholeness—for all of us.

The characteristics of ruthless, adversarial competition do not serve others. They serve the ego, and in our society, this ego-first way of thinking has, so far, been more prevalent. We are intoxicated with adversarial competitive rankings. The questions we ask come from the ego: How will I be judged or perceived? Will I be better than someone else? It's all about me—the very opposite of the serving characteristic—and it is all referenced from the outside, from the need for approval.

The leadership with which we are all too familiar is mainly informed by the ego that tends to separate—separateness thinking. Can my ego dominate your ego? It doesn't matter whether you're an employee or whether you're part of another company that provides the same services as mine. My job as a warrior-leader is to impose my will on all these other aspects of my domain: my politicians, my representative in Congress or Parliament, my lawyers, my accountants, my insurers, my customers, my suppliers. I need to win!

Life's most persistent and urgent question is, "What are you doing for others?"
Martin Luther King Jr.

The servant-leader transcends these ego-based issues by shifting to soul-inspired thinking that is based on the awareness that we are one, asking questions such as, How can I serve you better? or, How can I support you in a more loving way? The servant-leader has shifted emphasis from the ego to the soul, from the world viewed as separate parts to a world viewed as one. Although the personality remains part of who they are, it is not where they're anchored or where their primary focus resides. The servant-leader leads from the soul.

It is a fundamental principle of psychology that whatever we disown, cut off, or otherwise repress in our psyche becomes stronger and eventually will compel us to recognize its existence by surfacing in a distorted, exaggerated, or impulsive manner. Human evolution advances when we recognize that our need to fight rather than serve is part of our shadow that we have not yet owned, and then take steps to do so.

Violent and angry behavior is detrimental to the realization that we are part of one world, and it is hazardous to our health, too. Researchers have shown that angry, lonely men have a 72 percent greater chance of contracting gum disease (periodontitis).[11] Another study by Dr. Patricia P. Chang and colleagues from the Johns Hopkins University School of Medicine, published in the April 2002 issue of *Archives of Internal Medicine*, revealed that those with the highest levels of anger in response to stress were more than three times as likely to develop premature heart disease when compared with their less angry colleagues, and more than six times as likely to have a heart attack by age 55.

Another study, conducted by Buckinghamshire Chilterns University College in England and reported in the *Journal of Occupational and Environmental Medicine*, revealed that the systolic blood pressure of those studied increased about 13 points on average and their diastolic pressure increased six points on days spent working for a boss they thought was unfair. (The researchers point out that this increase is large enough to raise the risk of coronary heart disease by 16 percent and the risk of stroke by 38 percent.) Ruthless, adversarial, competitive, dysfunctional, separating behavior is counterproductive in almost every respect, including our health, and it alienates and frustrates those who must engage with it.

A Tale of Two Schools

All endeavors and professions are enhanced by the gift of service. Public education, for example, has often tended toward a standard-

---

11. The findings of researchers Anwar T. Merchant, DMD, ScD, and colleagues at Harvard School of Dental Medicine appear in the *Journal of the American Dental Association*, December 2003, vol 134: pp 1591–1596.

ized approach, particularly in the face of reduced budgets, teacher shortfalls, and decaying infrastructure. Public education is in crisis, especially affecting boys, a record number of whom are disengaged and alienated by the current system. Some U.S. statistics:

- From elementary through high school, boys receive lower report card grades than girls.
- Boys account for almost 75 percent of all school suspensions.
- Boys lag behind girls in reading and writing at all education levels.
- Boys excel in math and science.
- Boys are the majority of those identified for special education. Of that group, 70 percent are learning-disabled.
- Boys are nine times more likely than girls to suffer from hyperactivity. It is estimated that one in six boys (aged five to twelve) is diagnosed with attention deficit hyperactive disorder (ADHD).
- Boys commit 85 percent of school violence.
- African-American males are disciplined more often and more severely in school than any other minority group.[12]

We also know that learning styles are unique to each individual and that one size does not fit all. In fact, we serve students best by identifying the appropriate learning style for each one, along with the awareness of what inspires them, and then adapting the teaching to serve their needs, not the other way around, as we so often do now.

The Evander Childs High School in the Bronx is violent and unruly and an academic and social mess. Less than a third of its students graduate after four years, and even after seven, a mere 54 percent earn a diploma. Evander Childs has rented part of its

---

12. Mark Harris, final project for online course "Raising and Educating Boys: Developing Connections in a Changing World." The course was offered through the Gender and Diversity Institute at EDC. http://www.edc.org/GDI/develop.htm

second floor to an unusual tenant, the Bronx Laboratory School, which occupies just four classrooms and aspires to a graduation rate of 80 percent. It is an island of inspiration in a sea of fear. It isn't the buildings or the money that determines educational inspiration, it is the people and the way they teach—*the way they serve*—that makes the difference.

Teachers are the Guardians of Civilization.
Bertrand Russell

Marc Sternberg, Bronx Laboratory School's 32-year-old principal, has created a school that "expects a lot from our students, holds kids accountable for their performances, engages their parents as partners, and creates an instructional environment where learning doesn't necessarily happen in a 40-by-40-foot room but is a gateway to the world. So the emphasis is on project-based instruction. We have a 75-minute period. You can't teach a 75-minute period like a typical 45-minute period. It has to be students doing things and making something. That creation becomes the act of learning. We have monthly parent meetings, and there are lots of calls to and from parents."

Sternberg points out that another major difference from other schools is the level of involvement the school has in its students' personal lives. "When a student runs away from home or has an unexpected pregnancy or whatever, we are part of their families and they are a part of ours."

The emphasis on serving others and reinforcing a spirit of oneness is clear.

While studying at Princeton, Sternberg wrote his senior thesis on the civil rights movement in Baton Rouge, which became a study of the movement and its leadership, and why leaders failed and succeeded. Now he puts his theories into practice by serving students and parents—and by living the CASTLE Principles: with courage, authenticity, service, truth, love, and effectiveness.

Two schools with two different philosophies—separateness and oneness—in the same building, achieving almost diametrically opposing results.

The opportunity awaits us to adapt the educational system so that it meets the needs of students, tailoring teaching methods to serve their individual strengths, rather than their weaknesses, committing to inspiring them instead of intimidating them to learn, and therefore avoiding the very real risk of creating yet another lost generation. Students are customers, and the purpose of the organization—the educational system in this case—is to inspire and serve the needs of customer-students.

The leader as servant, then, is demonstrating emotional and spiritual maturity through the recognition that a desire to be aggressive can be recognized, owned, and tamed and the energy formerly invested in such behavior better directed into serving others. This is a personal breakthrough of enormous consequences and the beginning of inspiration for both the individual and those with whom he or she relates. It is a decision to move from separateness to oneness, and this decision always starts with individuals, who, in turn, change organizations, communities, and the world.

Serving by Listening

If you ask corporate leaders to describe the attributes of a good leader, they'll say it's all about being visionary, increasing shareholder wealth, delivering the numbers each quarter, beating the competition, and having a great strategy. But if you ask the followers, they will tell you that they want conscious leaders who, among other things, are compassionate and caring, just, fair, authentic, vulnerable, and truthful. They want leaders who have the courage to keep their promises and honor the people who work for them, who hold them in some form of sacred relationship, and who share information and rewards in a way that inspires them.

Leadership is the special quality which enables people to stand up and pull the rest of us over the horizon.

James L. Fisher

And so we have leaders and followers with completely different ideas of what's important in a leader.

What, then, is the leader's responsibility? It is to serve followers, and the dynamic of inspiration based on service leads to oneness between leader and other team members. This is what guides a team to greatness. It seems logical, therefore, that leaders would do well to first listen to the needs of their followers if they hope to meet them.

> My girlfriend says I never listen to her.
> I think that's what she said.
> *Drake Sather*

Members of a team often have a pretty good idea of what they would like to achieve in their organization. And if you ask them to dream and to stretch and to expand beyond their usual performance, they will often do just that. In fact, I have found that leaders frequently underestimate the potential and aspirations of followers.

I remember once when we were working with a client, one of the vice-presidents told me, "Spend the day with me walking around this organization, and I'll find $25 million that we could save—right away. No need to do research; no need for big consulting fees; no need to talk to anyone else. I already know. It's just that I don't have anyone who will listen to me and follow up." We serve best when we listen—and *then* act.

Marriage counselors will tell you that a breakdown in the capacity or desire to listen is often the fundamental reason for the collapse of a relationship. Educators believe that students who do poorly in school are often not being listened to by teachers.

Research by Howard B. Beckman, MD, and Richard M. Frankel, PhD, reported in *Annals of Internal Medicine*, shows that, on average, doctors interrupt patients in just 18 seconds after they begin to speak. More listening would increase our sense of being heard, of feeling whole and being healed—of being one with each other.

> When you listen to somebody else, whether you like it or not, what they say becomes part of you.
> *David Bohm*

Conversation has been described as a vocal competition in which the one who is catching his breath is called the listener. Generally, you aren't learning much when your lips are moving. We *talk* about the notion of listening more than we *practice* it. It is difficult to overestimate the importance of listening for the effective, inspiring leader.

Lessons in Listening from the Little Flower

> There is no Democratic or Republican way of cleaning the streets.
>
> *Fiorello LaGuardia*

Fiorello LaGuardia was the mayor of New York City during the dark days of the Great Depression and throughout World War II. Perhaps the most popular of all New York mayors, he was adored by his citizens, many of whom called him the Little Flower, because he was only five feet tall (plus a little bit) and always wore a carnation in his lapel. He was a mayor of the people, always listening to them, because he felt one with them. He rode the New York City fire trucks, raided city speakeasies with the police department, took entire orphanages to baseball games, and during the New York newspapers strike, read the Sunday funnies to the kids on the radio.

> If you can't feed a hundred people, then feed just one.
>
> *Mother Teresa*

LaGuardia was always looking for opportunities to listen. On a bitterly cold night in January of 1935, he entered a night court that served the poorest ward of the city. He dismissed the judge for the evening and took over the bench himself. One of the plaintiffs was a haggard street person charged with stealing a loaf of bread. She told LaGuardia that her daughter was sick and had been deserted by her husband and that her two grandchildren were starving.

But the shopkeeper from whom the bread had been stolen refused to drop the charges. "It's a real bad neighborhood, Your Honor," the man told the mayor. "She's got to be punished, to teach other people around here a lesson."

LaGuardia sighed. He turned to the woman and said, "I've got to punish you. The law makes no exceptions. Ten dollars or ten days in jail." As he was pronouncing the sentence, he reached into his pocket and extracted a bill and tossed it into his famous hat, saying, "Here is the ten-dollar fine, which I now remit; and furthermore I am going to fine everyone in this courtroom 50 cents for living in a town where a person has to steal bread so that her grandchildren can eat. Mr. Bailiff, collect the fines and give them to the defendant."

The following day, New York City newspapers reported that $47.50 was turned over to a bewildered woman who had stolen a loaf of bread to feed her starving grandchildren. Fifty cents of that amount was contributed by the grocery store owner himself. Some 70 petty criminals, including people with traffic violations, as well as New York City policemen, each of whom chipped in 50 cents, gave the mayor a standing ovation. The importance of listening!

You may be thinking that this is old stuff and that you have heard it all before, but what we hear most in our work with organizations, their leaders and teams, all over the world (it isn't even culturally based), is that *leaders do not listen*. We can say we have heard many times that we should listen more or tell the truth, but *doing* it is where we would be wise to place more of our attention. Conducting employee surveys does not, on its own, constitute listening. But hearing and *fully receiving* the thoughts, feelings, ideas, concerns, and emotions of others from them directly does.

Sometimes, we may forget that *I am responsible for what you hear.* We may have heard that we should inspire customers so well that they return again and again, but we all know many examples where this message may have been heard, but not practiced.

> If I have been of service, if I have glimpsed more of the nature and essence of ultimate good, if I am inspired to reach wider horizons of thought and action, if I am at peace with myself, it has been a successful day.
>
> *Alex Noble*

Peter Senge has observed that "to listen fully means to pay close attention to what is being said beneath the words. You listen not only to the 'music,' but to the essence of the person speaking. You listen not only for what someone knows, but for what he or she is. Ears operate at the speed of sound, which is far slower than the speed of light the eyes take in. Generative listening is the art of developing deeper silences in yourself, so you can slow your mind's hearing to your ears' natural speed, and hear beneath the words to their meaning."

Connecting the Dots to the Bottom Line

How does servant-leadership translate into better performance for the company? The answer is surprisingly simple: when we serve others, we inspire greatness from them by being one with them and adding to their wholeness.

One of our clients invokes what they call A Hundred Day Plan when they are behind budget, with expenses being too high and revenues being too low compared to budget or forecast. The Hundred Day Plan is intended to get the company back on track. Formerly, the company management would hear a message of separateness from the board:

> We cannot live for ourselves alone. Our lives are connected by a thousand invisible threads, and along these sympathetic fibers, our actions run as causes and return to us as results.
>
> *Herman Melville*

"We need your headcount to be reduced by two hundred people, and we need that to be done by next Thursday. How you do this is your problem. Just take care of it, because that's what is necessary to get back on budget."

This left people angry, isolated, and intimidated. It made them feel separate and alienated, and certainly not one with the organization's leadership. Now, managers are invited to a discussion, based on oneness, about how the situation can best be dealt with for all concerned. Today, managers may hear something quite different:

"You know how budgets work, and you know that we have to remain on budget, so how can we collaborate to make that happen? Do you think it might be a good idea to gather the entire team together and request their input and ideas on how we could do this?"

In this way, a plan is put together that serves the whole, one that is therefore even more effective in achieving the desired result, yet no one has been hurt or unfeelingly thrown into the (separate) ranks of the unemployed or required to fire others—one of the most extreme forms of separateness.

Try to forget yourself in service of others. For when we think too much of ourselves and our own interests, we easily become despondent. But when we work for others, our efforts return to bless us.

Sidney Powell

We have a choice in how we are going to achieve our objective of getting the company back on budget. We can do so with aggression or with service, by treating others as separate, or by treating them as one. A cynic might observe that the end result is the same, regardless of our approach. But even the most cynical can see that actions based on separateness have negative consequences, including lowered morale, quality, service, and greater absenteeism and staff turnover—and these have associated costs, to the bottom line, but also to the heart.

In the case of another client, for instance, who determined that their payroll was overweight by 300 people compared with budget, the leader asked the employees for creative suggestions regarding how the company could avoid the alternative of laying off 300 people. In a little more than two weeks, the 9,000 company employees came up with ideas, which, when fully implemented, generated more than enough extra revenue to cover the salaries of these 300 people.

People are creative. If you serve them by inviting them to join in conversation and then genuinely listen to them, they will feel engaged, served, and assured that they are being dealt with truthfully. When people are thus inspired, amazing outcomes can be expected. A servant-leader, faced with a challenge, sits with followers and asks them, "How can we resolve this problem together?" That's oneness.

At the Secretan Center, we practice preventive planning. From time to time, we get together and heartstorm (our term for "brainstorming") future scenarios, such as what we might do in the event that business fails to continue at its current pace. In our discussion, we ask our team members questions such as these: "What would happen if our business declined by 50 percent and there were no longer enough work for us all? What would you like to do then? We need to discuss this *before* it happens, not *when* it happens. Therefore, I'd like to know what your thoughts are while we do not have this problem. Would you take a sabbatical? Would you work part-time? Would you work for less money? Would you create new business? Do you have ideas for building revenues that would help to sustain us? Whatever the case, I'm giving you my commitment now that you will not be laid off. So I need to know, in giving you this commitment, what *your* commitment would be. And what would your contribution be at such a time?"

> The vocation of every man and woman is to serve other people.
>
> *Leo Tolstoy*

Another company that we work with—a large company in the energy business—found themselves, due to changing market conditions and redundant labor practices, with 50 percent more people than the business could legitimately sustain—3,500 people. Their solution was to treat their employees as one with the company and its future by asking them to visit their existing customers to determine the new services the company could provide to them, and for which they would be willing to pay. Using this research, the company created 60 new companies, retrained all of the redundant employees, and resituated all of them into new positions.

A different client, a hospital acquiring another, found their combined staffs to be 400 people more than required. To avoid any layoffs, they approached their local communities to ask for their support. If members of the community became customers, they explained, the increased revenues would enable the hospital to keep the extra employees on the payroll. The community rallied to their support, and everyone was able to keep their jobs.

Conscious leaders use courage and imagination to serve *everyone*—not just some of the separate constituents. Followers served this way are grateful and inspired and, in turn, they serve the organization and produce prosperity for the company, the shareholders, customers, suppliers, and the community.

What Goes Around Comes Around

Kirk Hoessle's office is a million acres of rugged green wilderness. Originally from Missouri, Kirk obtained a degree in Environmental Education and Outdoor Recreation, and then headed for the Alaskan wildlands. In 1982, he guided tent safaris for adventurers in Alaska's spectacular backcountry: Kenai National Wildlife Refuge, the Chugach National Forest, and Denali National Park. In those days, 50 fortunate beings soothed their souls each year on these wilderness raptures. Hoessle loved his work so much, he decided to acquire the company for which he worked, building it from those early beginnings into today's Alaska Wildland Adventures, an award-winning ecotourism firm that employs twelve year-round and 80 seasonal staff. Each year, the company operates tours for more than 1,000 guests visiting the Alaskan interior. Some stay in tents, but most overnight in authentic Alaskan log cabins. In 2005, Alaska Wildland Adventures counted former U.S. President Jimmy Carter and his wife among its guests.

Kirk's early experience as a guide and an employee in the company he now owns raised his awareness of how critical it is to the success of a business to serve its employees.

"I still remember what it was like to be an employee, and I know that my company's services absolutely depend on its employees and their interaction with customers," he says. "As an ecotourism company, we also recognize the oneness of people and the environment, and we serve them both as one."

When people are serving, life is no longer meaningless.
John W. Gardner

Hoessle has worked hard to serve the natural desire for trust and open communication with all employees. He practices open-book management, helping to build a sense of "family" through the honest disclosure of the company's financial information. A revenue-sharing plan is in place, and employees are surveyed annually for their ideas on improving operations, with the results being communicated at the beginning of each season. Hoessle also delegates much of the decision making to department managers, who in turn are encouraged to delegate decisions to committees and, where possible, individual colleagues. With access to financial information, employees can make informed spending decisions, arrange their own vacation schedules, and use their discretion on many matters. Alaska Wildland Adventures' seasonal employees enjoy their work so much that the majority of them return each year.

And their enjoyment is patently visible to outsiders. Glenda Denny heard about the company when she was working at a nearby hotel. Listening to the enthusiasm and passion of Alaska Wildland Adventures' guides convinced her to join the company.

"They were all so knowledgeable, and you could tell that they loved their jobs," she says.

Forty percent of guests are returning customers, some of whom have been taking trips with the company for 15 years.

The aftermath of 9/11 was devastating for Alaska Wildland Adventures, and Hoessle was forced to make difficult choices. But he involved his team in the decisions, inviting them to contribute their ideas to weathering the downturn. Rather than simply issuing pink slips to trim overhead, the company offered its employees the opportunity to take 30 days off work without pay.

Some chose to take their time off all at once, while others chose to work four-day weeks. Hoessle gave loans to those facing hardship as a result of the new schedules. Employees were encouraged to make use of the different lodges the company operates during the off-season. Kirk wanted to be sure the company was helping them during these hard times.

Greater challenges were to come. Early during the summer of 2003, lightning struck a designated wilderness area located on a remote mountain slope only two miles away from Kenai Backcountry Lodge, owned and operated by Alaska Wildland Adventures, causing a smoldering fire. In Alaska's designated wilderness, a wildfire is considered to be a natural part of the ecosystem and is allowed to burn unless there is a danger of its going out of control or the fire appears to threaten structures or critical areas. So, the fire caused by the lighting strike was left to smolder.

That summer was unusually dry, and eventually Kenai Backcountry Lodge's primary water supply, based on a spring-fed stream, dried up for the very first time in the company's history. This was the first signal to management that there was a high risk that the fire would get out of control.

Hoessle's team phoned the Alaskan State fire management agencies almost daily in late July and early August, requesting action to fight the fire, but there was no immediate response because the agencies did not accurately assess the fire's devastating potential.

On August 10, Hoessle received a phone call in his Girdwood office, about a three-hour drive and boat ride from Kenai Backcountry Lodge. The call was from a resident on the far side of the lake across from the lodge, advising that smoke could be seen billowing up from the shore. Alarmed, Hoessle called the lodge manager, who, after riding a boat out into the lake, confirmed that the fire was indeed raging down toward the lake—and the Kenai Backcountry Lodge was directly in its path. Hoessle's team immediately evacuated the eight-cabin lodge, making alternative arrangements for the guests.

After contacting Kenai National Wildlife Refuge, responsible for alerting the Alaska State fire control, Hoessle and two other staff members went home to pack sleeping bags, appropriate clothing, chainsaws, and any equipment they thought might be useful. Then they drove off toward Kenai Backcountry Lodge. There, with the help of lodge staff, they used the lodge's own hoses and emergency pumps to wet down the buildings. They also created a fire-break around the lodge property by cutting down trees and bushes in a fire-break line. Late in the evening, an eight-person fire-fighting crew arrived by boat. But, disappointingly for Hoessle and his team, they left again when winds kicked up, creating additional danger, and advised Hoessle and his staff to leave the site, too.

Realizing that he would need to mobilize additional people to help save the lodge, if at all possible, Kirk put in a call late that evening to Kevin McDermott, a former employee, who now owned a construction firm. Without hesitation, Kevin agreed to take his crew up to Kenai Backcountry Lodge to help fight the fire. He also contacted another former employee, Dennis Weber, who in turn called his brother Mike and his wife Jen. Dennis, Mike, and Jen wasted no time, leaving that evening. They packed their own chainsaws and other equipment and drove through the night to reach the site by early morning. All of the people in this group, including Mike, Jen, and Kevin's crew, were former employees of Alaska Wildland Adventures.

From six in the morning until noon, 18 employees and ex-employees worked as one to fight the fire, and only then did the first firefighter crews arrive. The employee crew worked all day to cut the fire line. No one asked if, or how much, they would be paid.

"A week later," Hoessle remembers, "I handed them all checks, and I had to really work hard to get them to take the money."

Kenai Backcountry Lodge, a crucial component of Alaska Wildland Adventures' business, was saved thanks to the efforts of former employees whose commitment to the company did not end when they chose to pursue different careers.

Having started out as a guide in the company, Kirk is very much aware of how serving others creates staff satisfaction and effectiveness. And others on his team have shared the same experience. Kyle Kelly began as a driver and was promoted to trip leader and then program manager. He is now responsible for all of Alaska Wildland Adventures' operations.

In the long run we get no more than we have been willing to risk giving.
Sheldon Kopp

Hoessle knows that team members need to be respected, honored, and heard—to be served. He involves his staff in the decision processes on an ongoing basis. He believes in managing for results and not demoralizing people by micro-managing them. He upholds the principle that everyone respects everyone else, even when there is disagreement, and that it is important to first understand before one tries to be understood. Authentic listening is an important aspect of this practice.

"People work here because they are attracted to our cause and environmental beliefs," he says. "They stay because they are treated well."

Serving others is always a good investment.

Look again at those words, "They stay because they are treated well." That's true for employees, customers, spouses, parishioners, partners, friends, and citizens. Serving others with the awareness that we are all connected, all interdependent, all one, is the best investment we can make in ourselves—because we are part of the one, too.

Practicing Oneness by Reclaiming Our Passion for Service

Serving others, our environment, and a higher purpose—our destiny—is the reason for living. When we serve, we inspire, and when we serve,

A man wrapped up in himself makes a very small package.
Benjamin Franklin

we lead. And when we serve, inspire, and lead this way, we become one with those whom we serve. Reflect on these questions as you deepen your commitment to serving others:

- In order to serve, we must first listen—do you listen *to hear*?
- Do you choose to serve rather than to compete?
- It has been said that anger is like drinking poison and expecting the other person to die. Have you let go of anger, so that you are able to serve?
- Has fear been banished in your work and personal environments, so that service can flourish?
- Do you always attempt to heal and make a conscious effort never to wound?
- Have you replaced fear and aggression with service and compassion?
- When we serve others more, we add to our own growth. How are you becoming a better servant of others—and therefore growing yourself?
- Would your colleagues consider you to be a "servant-leader"?
- Would your former and current colleagues "drive through the night to put out your fire"?
- Are you serving in ways that contribute to the oneness of all people and the planet?

BOTTOM LINE

Why do we need Service?
Because Service is a gift to others that makes
competition, aggression, and self-interest irrelevant.
We are one.

REFLECTIONS TO INSPIRE GROWTH IN SERVICE

Describe one of the highest moments of Service in your life—when you were at your personal best, Serving the needs of others:

_____

_____

_____

_____

_____

Describe a current situation in your life that, in your heart, you know would be enhanced through the practice of greater Service to others. It is within you already, so how would you apply the same level of Service, described in your own example above, to this current situation?

_____

_____

_____

_____

_____

_____

Those who bring sunshine into the lives of others, cannot keep it from themselves.

James Barrie

8

TRUTHFULNESS

THERE IS AN OLD RIDDLE that goes like this: A traveler comes to a fork in a path that leads to two villages. In one village, the people always tell lies, and in the other village, the people always tell the truth. The traveler needs to visit a relative who lives in the village where everyone always tells the truth. Two sisters are standing in the middle of the fork between the villages. One always lies, and the other always tells the truth, but the traveler cannot determine which one is which. With just one carefully phrased question, the traveler is able to obtain a response from one of the sisters, who indicates which path to follow. What question did the traveler ask?

Give up? Here's the answer: He asked either sister, "Which path would *she* (pointing to the other sister) say leads to the village where people always tell the truth?" and then he took the opposite path to the one she suggested.

But here is an even more important question: Which sister would you rather have as your friend? The one who lies, or the one who tells the truth?

Devaluing the Currency of Truth

Researchers have shown that people tell an average of 13 lies a week. Another study suggests that lying occurs in almost two-thirds of conversations. About three-quarters of us "doctor" our résumés and, according to one study, between 20 and 30 percent of business managers have written fraudulent internal reports. In a large study of biomedical research scientists, Brian Martinson of Health Partners Research Foundation in Minneapolis and Melissa Anderson and Raymond de Vries of the University of Minnesota report that 33 percent of respondents admitted to committing at least one professionally dubious act in the previous three years. A little over 15 percent of the respondents admitted to "changing the design, methodology or results of a study in response to pressure from a funding source."

The elegance of honesty needs no adornment.
Merry Browne

Though any one of these incidents in itself might not be significant, repetitive, insidious lapses of integrity do have the effect, in time, of undermining our faith and trust in our institutions—and worse, each other. Perpetrating "dubious acts" in biomedical science to ensure the continuing flow of research funding is another demonstration of the illusion of separateness, which, in this case, could have significant negative impact on the health and lives of millions, all because of a lack of awareness of our interconnectedness—our oneness.

We used to live much more closely together, in small communities, where the impact of telling lies could be much greater. The community was one, and lying quickly became a community issue, not just a personal matter. Although we have temporarily lost that sense of community, it is returning, and with the assistance of the digital age, we are restoring our collective sense of conscience. It is becoming more difficult to hide our lies from digital eyes, and therefore the consequences of lying pose a rising disincentive. In a certain sense, the Internet has become a digital conscience.

Marge, it takes two to lie. One to lie and one to listen.

Homer Simpson

In some of our seminars and retreats, we ask our participants to complete a questionnaire listing a number of statements and invite them to rate the applicability of each to their lives. The scale runs from zero to ten, with zero representing "no," and ten representing "yes." One of these statements is, "I always tell the truth." Most people respond by marking a number somewhere in the upper digits along the scale, typically around eight or nine. We find very few tens, but we often see nine-and-a-half.

Then we ask, "What do you mean, nine-and-a-half, given that the statement is, 'I *always* tell the truth'?" Someone will say, "Well, what I meant was that I *nearly* always tell the truth. Sometimes, I may not tell the truth, or I omit the truth by not saying it. Or perhaps the truth might be really irritating to someone, in which case I might not say the whole truth, or sometimes I don't want to hurt someone's feelings, but otherwise, most of the time, I do tell the truth."

Every violation of truth is not only a sort of suicide in the liar, but is a stab at the health of human society.

Ralph Waldo Emerson

We explain, "Then your answer should be zero, shouldn't it? The statement says, 'I *always* tell the truth.' Your answer to that could only be either yes or no, not something in between."

This gentle ruse highlights how we play fast and loose with the truth in work and life. The fact that we get these fudged responses is an indication that we've diluted our standards of truth, and that many of us are quite prepared to give a compromising answer because we have compromised the meaning of truth. We think that this is okay, and that we are being truthful if we tell the truth most of the time. After all, we argue, everyone does it, and to do otherwise would be naïve in today's world. And so we have devalued the currency of truth.

The Varieties of Deception

There are many ways in which we are not being truthful. Every time we put together a budget that is not truthful and honest, where we hide items and mask others under different labels, departments or categories, we are not telling the truth. In fact, when I ask participants in our retreats if they have ever seen a truthful budget, they usually laugh, as if such an idea were charmingly old-fashioned.

There are three truths:
my truth, your truth, and the truth.
Chinese proverb

Similarly, we are seldom fully truthful in advertising, product descriptions, or labeling. Among ingredients listed on a label, for instance, we might see "sugar" near the top, and then "glucose" or "fructose" listed separately. But glucose and fructose are simply different forms of sugar, and it's just a crafty way in which companies, in effect, avoid truthfulness with their customers about the total sugar content of a product.

I once suggested to the management of one of the world's largest food companies that they consider placing a label on their products saying, "We tell the truth. Here is a complete and accurate listing of what's inside this product..." I had a strong hunch that this might create an enormous increase in consumer interest and loyalty, especially for the nutritionally conscious, who would know that they could trust the brands of this organization unconditionally, because the truth was guaranteed.

The executives thought this was a brilliant idea, but after running it through various internal departments, they decided that since it would be such a radical change to the rules of the game, it would create insurmountable complications for their dealings with advertising agencies, distributors, manufacturers, suppliers, consumers, regulators, and insurers. It would be too daunting a challenge for them to raise the bar of truthfulness this high.

"Our lawyers," they said, "would be all over us, telling us that we can't do this and we can't do that—we'd have one lawsuit after another."

They concluded they were unable to follow through on this suggestion because their investment in subterfuge and untruthful communications was simply too deep and long-standing. Thus, they reconfirmed their commitment to continuing falsehoods.

In 2005, when McDonald's Corp. announced that the company would display nutrition information on the packaging for most of its menu items beginning in 2006, the company's share price immediately *rose 3 percent*. We are yearning for the truth, and truthfulness is *good*, not bad, for business.

Labels can be a company's greatest asset or its greatest liability. The tobacco industry stood accused of denying the addictive nature of cigarettes and that they caused cancer, and supporting these claims with spurious data. Ultimately, the tobacco industry lost its case and was fined more than $250 billion for misleading Americans. (That may seem like a big number, but to appreciate just how big it is, if you started counting out loud, it would take you more than 7,500 years to reach it.) If the tobacco industry had simply printed warnings on its packages—in other words, told the truth—when they were well aware that tobacco kills, they might have been able to make a plausible defense. Telling the truth might have been far less expensive than a campaign of lies. Many people would have smoked anyway. There are no actions without consequences. We are one.

Truth: The Greatest Profit Booster Known

Telling the truth could be the single greatest profit generator in corporate history. I estimate that some 20 percent of the workforce today is involved in checking up on the other 80 percent, making sure that company rules and regulations are followed, that the law is respected, that expenses are authentic, that budgets are met, and that there's honesty and integrity in the countless processes and procedures around which companies are structured.

This means that in an organization of 10,000 people, somewhere in the order of 2,000 are responsible for ensuring that their other 8,000 colleagues follow the rules, and they do this through audits, budget control, compliance, expense approval, and so on. If we assume that each person costs the company an average of $50,000 a year, including salaries, benefits, and overhead, the total cost is a staggering $100 million annually. But if we started a system-wide initiative of truthfulness, and if we were only 50 percent successful in doing so, then we could theoretically save 1,000 jobs—half the people who are checking up on the other 8,000.

We could then retrain those 1,000 people to do productive work, such as meeting the needs of customers better, inspiring employees, lowering staff turnover, creating innovative new products or services, and making quality legendary. These people are already on the payroll, and if their energy and enthusiasm (not to mention their cost to the organization of $50 million) could be redirected toward more productive endeavors that *make* money, rather than activities that *cost* money, they could contribute even more significantly toward organizational transformation, effectiveness, and profitability.

So, when we say that we can't find enough quality people and that companies suffer from staff shortages, let's think again! There are plenty of good people, but we've put them in the wrong jobs— jobs they undertake because we are not doing the right thing to start with: we're not telling the truth, and we have consequently settled for the mediocrity that results from a lack of truthfulness. Truth is a powerful economical tool. In fact, there is probably no single initiative that could boost profits more than a radical commitment to truthfulness—not Kaizen, Six Sigma, cost-cutting, TQM, nor any other of the popular "profit improvement programs."

When Mary Cusack was invited to start up a $50-million packaging plant for Procter & Gamble's Light Duty Liquids (Dawn,

Joy, Ivory brands), she realized that the project was riddled with distrust and dishonesty. Working with HR manager Don White, she initiated a truth-telling process inspired by Brad Blanton (author of *Radical Honesty*) and Will Schutz (author of *The Human Element*).

"We got people to look each other in the eye, share their appreciation, state their resentments, get over them and move on," Cusack reports. She was personally able to share "all the information and opinions that I based my decisions on. I became vulnerable in front of my people. As a woman in a manufacturing plant, I wasn't supposed to show emotions. But it worked to my advantage."

A dramatic improvement in decision-making speed and productivity resulted from this courageous truth-telling. Although it usually takes 18 to 24 months to build a plant, Cusack did the job in six months and developed new bottle designs in this time, too.

"We saved 12 to 18 months," she says. "That's $10 million."

We have it backwards: we think that telling the truth will cost money and get us into trouble. The opposite is true.

We Get What We Expect

The assumption underlying corporate controls and expense approval procedures is that people will not be truthful unless their spending is verified and audited. As a CEO, I start with the assumption that everyone in our organization is truthful. When our colleagues incur work-related expenses, they submit the necessary vouchers describing how much they have spent, and we reimburse them. Why can't it be that simple everywhere? Why do we require that expense reports be completed in triplicate and approved by different managers?

If someone in our organization says they require an afternoon away from work so they can take their child to the doctor, we don't ask them to prove it by requesting "evidence" in the form of a doctor's certificate. We trust people, and we want them to be whole. An employee who is worrying about their sick child will not be as productive or as loyal as one who isn't. Trusted employees feel whole and are therefore able to be more present and inspired. Our philosophy is that if a trusted colleague (that is, *all* colleagues) needs time to look after personal affairs, then they should have that time. There is no need for them to lie.

We are sometimes asked if people abuse a system that trusts them unconditionally. But our experience has been that people don't abuse systems in which they're trusted. If everyone knows, as they do in our organization, that if they need time off for any reason, all they have to do is ask for it, and if they can have all the time they need, then why would they abuse the system that gives them this flexibility? We find that they don't.

In an inspired team, with an appreciation for the concept of oneness, there is a commitment to one another to serve and inspire. Lying doesn't achieve that, and is therefore seldom practiced in high-performance teams. Inspired team members don't cheat or lie to their colleagues. They know that if they let others down, they let themselves down, because they are one.

Much of this has to do with getting what we expect. If we expect people to be honest, truthful, and straightforward, we will attract honest, truthful, and straightforward people into our lives—and as leaders, into our organizations. In time, this transforms the culture of the organization and its relationships with suppliers, customers, and employees. Around 2 percent of the time, this confidence will be misplaced and people will let us down. This can be painful and expensive. But we need to live our lives in anticipation and celebration of the 98 percent, not the 2 percent, working on our strengths, not our weaknesses.

> Truth exists, only falsehood has to be invented.
> *Georges Braque*
> *(Pensées sur l'Art)*

Some years ago, in the Little Venice area of Los Angeles, a restaurant was failing to build its fledgling business. They surmised that their prices were too high. So the restaurant owners implemented a new policy. They removed the prices from the menu and asked patrons to pay whatever they thought the meal was worth. The result was an *increase* in the average bill of 35 percent. In what might seem to be a counterintuitive result, patrons paid more for their meals than the prices on the previous menu had indicated. Assume that people are essentially generous in nature and they will be. It's called intentionality.

In Kleinburg, Ontario, there's a little garden café called Mr. McGregor's House, named after the character in Beatrix Potter's story of Peter Rabbit. The restaurant operates on the trust principle. Patrons select food and drinks from the buffet and take them to their table. No one keeps tabs on what or how much people take. At the end of the their stay, patrons go to the cash desk, where they describe to the staff all the items that they've consumed, and their bill is then totaled and paid.

One of my colleagues recently lined up to pay her bill, behind someone who was there for the first time. This person asked the owner of the café, who was standing at the cash desk, if people were always honest and paid for what they had consumed. She said that by and large, they did. The patron then commented, "You're still in business, so I suppose your customers really are honest." This restaurant owner expects all her patrons to be worthy of her trust, and she gets what she expects.

Rewarding Truth

Why, then, are we so often afraid to tell the truth? Is it because we've been conditioned to expect a negative reaction or even punishment? We not only get what we expect, we also get what we reward. And if we aspire to create organizations, institutions, families, and a society that rewards truth, we will need to implement a complete redesign of the systems so that they support truthfulness.

Non-truthfulness is rampant in all parts of society, and omissions of the truth are as frequent as falsehoods.

In her memoirs, Nancy Reagan relates how Vice-President George H. Bush approached her with concerns about Chief of Staff Donald Regan. Mrs. Reagan said she wished he'd tell her husband, but Bush replied that it was not his role to do so.

"That is exactly your role," she retorted.

A culture of truthfulness is facilitated by changing the corporate infrastructure, so that it no longer rewards those who lie at the expense of those who don't, and by leaders who set the standard.

This requires fundamental changes to the compensation, personal review, and performance appraisal systems, as well as budgets and many other processes. This, of course, entails a considerable investment of time and energy and is not accomplished overnight. Commitment and patience are required to implement a new corporate structure and the accompanying processes that lead to a culture of truthfulness. But the rewards, which derive from the profound ways in which human dignity and the sacredness of the soul are acknowledged, lead to lower stress, absenteeism, staff turnover, customer complaints, and improved bottom line, making it well worth the effort.

Truth Inspires

Liars sadden and disappoint us. They frighten and hurt us. But champions of the truth inspire us and brighten our lives with hope. They show us that there is a higher ground upon which we can all stand.

Bernie Bredschneider, a high-school teacher and athletic coach at Mayfield Secondary School in Caledon, Ontario, Canada, shows us how. He coaches the outstanding Mayfield Mavericks girls' swim team, which has a long history of winning championships at major sports events.

During the winter of 2005, the team trained in their usual,

dedicated way to prepare for the OFSAA (Ontario Federation of School Athletic Association) championships in March. They knew that, with the right commitment, practice, and attitude, they could win the OFSAA Banner.

"For the thousand or so kids that show up," says coach Bredschneider, "an OFSAA championship is just like the Olympics. It's an amazing event. These kids really come to excel. They put everything out, and they give everything they've got, to come away from that experience knowing they have given their best."

In the final of the March 2005 championship, the girls in Bernie's team were matched against the best teams from other schools, all competing for the gold medal that would be claimed by the winner. It was an important race for another reason. The points earned would contribute to the totals necessary for the school to win the overall title at the end of the two-day competition—a prospect that, with their characteristic focus and aspiration, would be well within their reach.

Suddenly, in a moment marked by high tension, one of the four girls left the block a fraction of a second before the swimmer ahead of her had touched the wall. It was a team's worst fear: a false start. Gasps and groans of disappointment could be heard from the Mayfield coaches and athletes who noticed the error. The feelings of stress and uncertainty rose as the race continued to the finish. The team was on tenterhooks as they anxiously awaited a ruling from the officials.

But luck was with them. With eight relay teams competing simultaneously, only one of the three officials had noticed the incident. The judges conferred on the team's performances and concluded that none of them had seen anything to clearly disqualify the swimmer, and awarded the gold medal to Mayfield.

"That's the rule in swimming," says Bredschneider. "You have to have a clear view of the infraction. If you can't say with absolute certainty that you saw a breach of the rules, then no disqualification can be made, and this is what happened in our case. Their uncertainty steered them towards avoiding a disqualification—and a decision in our favor."

But coach Bredschneider's team, including his assistant coaches and swimmers, knew differently—they were almost certain that there had been a false start.

As Bredschneider said later, "There was a little bit of doubt in our minds, because when you're at an angle looking from 25 meters away, it's possible to misjudge. It was not until later that day, when I replayed the relay takeover in my mind, that it became clear to me that we should have been disqualified."

Following the official ruling in the team's favor, the Mavericks began justifying it, feeling that it was the hand of fate compensating for a particularly poor call made against one of their swimmers four years earlier.

"We kind of headed for the door with our tails between our legs, ready to walk away from this having accepted that we got away with something," recalls Bredschneider.

As they left the pool, one of the officials remarked to a Mayfield coach, "Yeah, you dodged a bullet."

Bernie slept fitfully that night. As he pondered the day, he realized that the gold medal and the team banner that Mayfield stood to win would remain forever tainted. This outcome did not sit well with him. The next morning, he held a meeting with his coaches, and they decided unanimously to propose returning the gold medal.

At the team breakfast, Bredschneider and his coaches engaged the four girls in a separate conversation, telling them that there was no doubt in their minds that they should have been disqualified, and suggesting that the team consider returning the medal. With little discussion, the girls agreed with their coaches.

"We had no dissenters," says Bernie, "and I'm certain we all knew in our hearts that this was the right thing to do."

As was expected, the officials refused to reverse the decision. Undeterred, Bredschneider requested a meeting with the coaches

No pleasure is comparable to the standing upon the vantage ground of Truth.

Francis Bacon

⌒

of the second-, third-, and fourth-place teams, telling them that Mayfield wanted to turn over their gold medal to the second-place team, who would then pass theirs to the third-place team, making the fourth-place team the bronze medal winner.

"There was an astonished look around the room," recalls Bredschneider, "but everyone eventually agreed. We went on with the rest of the swim meet. Kind and compassionate words were exchanged between the schools involved, and the balance of the program was uneventful."

But word of the incident soon reached the editorial offices of a major local newspaper, the *Toronto Star*, which dispatched one of their sports reporters to interview Bredschneider and his team.

"The response to this story was nothing short of amazing," says Bredschneider. "For several months after this incident, I was receiving phone calls and letters from many people, including Ontario's Minister of Education, a former Speaker of the House of Commons, the Premier of Ontario, and the President of Husky Canada in Bolton."

The relay swimmers received recognition from the Canadian Olympic Committee and from local universities and were invited to be guest speakers at a breakfast for Horizons for Youth. Many from the Mayfield community and surrounding towns also wrote letters and made phone calls. Letters from Mayfield alumni arrived from as far away as Milwaukee.

Bernie Bredschneider was in awe when he witnessed the power of a simple act of truthfulness to inspire not only an entire community, but also countless others who heard about it.

The sustained influx of positive feedback and encouragement from within the Mayfield community, and beyond, surprised and profoundly inspired all those who were close to the relay team.

"What astounded me was the sheer number of people who

were touched by this and felt compelled to share their reaction with us," says Bernie. "It was simply a matter of doing what we knew was right, but it seemed to be a breath of fresh air in the world of sports, where people have come to expect selfishness, foul play, drugs, and money issues."

While Bredschneider was surprised by the overwhelming response to this simple act, the four girls were even more surprised. "I think that in their youth and innocence, following their hearts to do what was selfless and right was easy—it's something most of us are born with, an innate sense—and it's helped them to get this far in their young lives," he says. "I sincerely hope that the many heartfelt messages of encouragement they received from the adult world will always serve to remind them of how easy it is to fill the world with love—a life lesson for us all, and one that gives me hope."

> The truth is always exciting. Speak it, then. Life is dull without it.
> *Pearl Buck*

We are not separate, we are one. When we lie and assume that no one notices, we are deluding ourselves. The truth is, truth inspires.

Practicing Oneness by Reclaiming Our Truthfulness

If we are untruthful, then we are no longer one with the truth, because we have separated ourselves from it. If we are not being truthful, how can we inspire or lead? We can do much to become more effective leaders by honoring the spirit of oneness through ending the practice of being untruthful. Here are some thoughts to help you implement your intentions to practice greater truthfulness—to practice the level of truthfulness that you have often achieved in the past—and make it the standard practice now throughout your life:

Creating a Truthful Culture

- A team cannot be built on a foundation of deceit.
- Truthfulness is the cornerstone of good chemistry with people because it builds trust, which leads to consistency.
- Truthfulness is an act of love—and being untruthful is the opposite.
- In organizations, truthfulness is a value *and* a system.
- Truthfulness requires regular maintenance.

Making Truth-Telling Safe

- There will be no recriminations against, or punishment of, truth-tellers.
- We tell the truth in a helpful and positive way. We will endeavor never to wound with the truth.
- This is the beginning of our mutual truth-telling. What has gone before is irrelevant.

Some Questions to Guide Us towards Greater Truthfulness

- Do we tell the truth to each other?
- What are the costs of being untruthful?
- Is it safe to tell the truth?
- Do others feel safe enough with me to tell me the truth?
- Am I true to myself?
- Do others know me as a truth-teller?
- Can I be more effective through truth-telling?
- Am I truthful with those closest to me—my family and friends?
- Do you love me enough to tell me the truth?

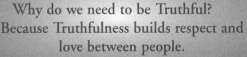

BOTTOM LINE

Why do we need to be Truthful?
Because Truthfulness builds respect and
love between people.
We are one.

REFLECTIONS TO INSPIRE GROWTH IN TRUTHFULNESS

Describe one of the most Truthful moments in your life—a time when you were at your personal Truthful best:

_____

_____

_____

_____

_____

Describe a current situation in your life that, in your heart, you know would be enhanced if you practiced greater Truthfulness. It is within you already, so how would you apply the same level of Truthfulness, described in your own example above, to this current situation?

_____

_____

_____

_____

_____

Truth sits upon the lips of dying men.
Matthew Arnold

9

LOVE

I DEFINE LOVE AS *the place where my heart touches your heart and adds to who we both are as persons.* When we connect with others heart to heart, it doesn't mean that we are weak, and it does not require anyone to "submit" to someone or "give up" anything. In a dialogue that comes from the sweetness of your heart to that of another, there are only winners, not losers—there is, simply, oneness.

Conscious leaders who have the courage to be humble, forgiving, and loving—and therefore authentic—are much more inspiring and effective leaders, because they use their hearts to engage the hearts of others. There is deep wisdom and power in opening our heart and using it to relate to others. These are the relationships that inspire, because they are heart-to-heart and cause us to feel and connect as one.

Considering that the greatest human need is to love and be loved, it is disconcerting that so many leaders have themselves lost their connection to myth, mystery, and magic and therefore to their hearts. Rediscovering love could inspire them and others.

The Psychopathology of Corporations

Twenty years ago, the director of the country's largest psychiatric institution shocked me with the observation that 30 percent of corporate leaders, if assessed clinically, would be diagnosed as sociopathic. This set me on a search for more information, and I came across the work of corporate psychologist Paul Babiak and Robert D. Hare, professor emeritus in psychology at the University of British Columbia. Their definition of a psychopath includes these criteria:

1. Comes across as smooth, polished, and charming.
2. Turns most conversations around to a discussion of him- or herself.
3. Discredits or puts down others in order to build up own image and reputation.
4. Lies to co-workers, customers, or business associates with a straight face.
5. Considers people he or she has outsmarted or manipulated as dumb or stupid.
6. Opportunistic; hates to lose, plays ruthlessly to win.
7. Comes across as cold and calculating.
8. Acts in an unethical or dishonest manner.
9. Has created a power network in the organization and uses it for personal gain.
10. Shows no regret for making decisions that negatively affect the company, shareholders, or employees.

This might sometimes be a summary of the character (or lack thereof) of a few corporate executives or a profile of the behavior of some organizations, because, in many ways, these are the behaviors so admired and rewarded in separateness thinking.

The average score based on the expanded version of Dr. Hare's profile, when applied to incarcerated male offenders in North America, is 23.3 out of a possible 40. A score of around 20 qualifies as "moderately psychopathic." Thankfully for most of us, only 1 percent of the general population would score 30 or above, which is "highly psychopathic"—the range for the most violent offenders.

But more intriguing is the notion that a corporation is built to be sociopathic. The list above could easily stand as a proxy for the profile of some corporations when they ruthlessly seek their own selfish interests—shareholder value, for instance—without regard for the harms they cause to others resulting from separateness thinking, such as environmental damage or employment insecurity, or the risks to the health and safety of customers. A corporation is legally mandated to make a profit, and that commitment may sometimes mean sacrificing the public good. Public companies have even been sued because, in the opinion of some shareholders, they favored another priority over maximizing profit, such as protecting the environment, with a consequent, short-term cost to the bottom line. A paranoid and driven focus can sometimes foster behavior in others that they would never bring to their homes and families. Using the list of characteristics above, how do you assess your organization?

Of course, I don't mean to suggest that all organizations or their leaders are psychopathic. But when the behaviors listed above are admired and celebrated in organizations, a few can change—even spoil—the world of work for many. In effect, our media, compensation systems, human resource policies, management education, leadership development, and career development programs support and encourage the tendency to psychopathic behavior in modern corporate life—this is how separateness metastasizes.

Dr. Babiak's research began almost accidentally. He had been invited to advise a major corporation in Colorado. His assignment was to assess an underperforming management team. A new member had joined its ranks. Morale was low, conflict high.

Initially, Babiak was charmed by the fast-talking guy at the center of the problem.

Says Babiak, "He came across very sincere and modest, and I only came to realize there was something going on when I got the results of the assessments that were being done, and I found quite a discrepancy. A number of people really, really liked him, and that included some of the higher-level people, I must say. And a number of people really despised him, really thought he was evil. One person referred to him as a 'snake.' It was only later, really, after the assignment ended and I consulted with Bob Hare, that I saw the light. Bob had sent me the PCL-R, or the Psychopathy Checklist, which he had developed while studying psychopaths in prison samples.

"He came out high on the conning and manipulation side of the PCL-R equation and middle-of-the-road on the anti-social behavior side. Thus he was able to hide his manipulations from the view of those around him, yet he exerted undue influence, negative influence, on the group."

We hear much these days about the requirements for leaders to deal with breathtaking change—to eat or be eaten—that "only the paranoid survive." This, Babiak thinks, is the perfect ground for a person with psychopathic tendencies.

"The psychopath has no difficulty dealing with the consequences of rapid change; in fact, he or she thrives on it," Babiak claims. "Organizational chaos provides both the necessary stimulation for psychopathic thrill-seeking and sufficient cover for psychopathic manipulation and abusive behavior."

Another study, by research psychologists Belinda Board and Katarina Fritzon of the University of Surrey, showed that the executives they interviewed and compared to criminals and psychiatric patients were even more likely to be superficially charming, egocentric, insincere, and manipulative, and just as likely to be grandiose, exploitative, and lacking in empathy.

Based on this research, Board and Fritzon classified the businesspeople they studied as "successful psychopaths" and the criminals as "unsuccessful psychopaths"—the latter being distinguished mainly by their tendency to be more impulsive and physically aggressive.

The Origins of a Loveless Outlook

In my work, I frequently meet men (and sometimes women, too) who tell me that their parents, especially their fathers, never told them they loved them. They found it especially hard to say to their sons, "I love you." Sadly, many of them may go to their graves without ever having said those words. They are too afraid to do so—afraid of showing their vulnerability or opening their hearts because of the conditioning they experienced during their early family years. As boys living in these situations, craving love and acceptance without gaining them, many strained to earn this affection through accomplishment—household chores, musical, artistic, athletic, or academic achievement—like a retriever fetching a stick to earn a treat. Many found that this method of gaining acceptance was the only way that worked for them. Thus, a lifelong pattern became established.

Love is the difficult realization that something other than oneself is real.
Iris Murdoch

Over and over again, I hear the same story: "My dad never told me he loved me." This pain represents a hole in the soul, a void which many leaders strive to fill with organizational accomplishments. Twenty years later, these boys, now men, practice the same system—the only one they have ever known; the only one that they have ever found to be successful. Unconsciously, these leaders provide a framework and a cultural environment that repeats and deepens their childhood dysfunctions. Instead of inspiring others to greatness, they create teams, organizations, and countries that are just as dysfunctional as they are.

There is an opportunity here to transcend this pain, to use the experience as a way to grow, rather than as a pattern to be repeated. History repeats itself because no one listens the first time. Maya Angelou has said, "History, despite its wrenching pain, cannot be unlived, but if faced with courage, need not be lived again." If we can mature in this way, then we can move from a fear-based leadership style to one that comes from the heart. Then, paradoxically, we will receive untold amounts of love.

In his book *Sweating From Your Eyes: Emotional Fitness for Men* (Fresh Wind Press, 2005), Dave Loney writes that he never knew how much his 70-year-old father loved him until one day, as they were both cutting wood in a forest, Dave was struck on the head and shoulder by a large limb that dislodged and fell from a dead tree.

"Barely conscious," he writes, "I heard my father running over to me. 'David! Oh! My David. Oh! God! My David.'

"I wanted to lie there, feigning unconsciousness, listening to him grieve, listening to his words communicating his love. It was a healing moment…Fortunately, I only had the wind knocked out of me…Sometimes we just have to be hit by a tree."

Although the scars of the challenging relationship with his father have taken time to heal, Dave resolved to transform his painful experiences and raise his own children in an environment of unconditional love and honor. He and his immensely supportive wife have three grown children who have blossomed into healthy, productive, and emotionally fit members of the community who won't need to wait for a tree to fall on them to hear and understand how much their father loves them.

It takes courage to tell someone you love them, and to be a loving person—far more courage than it takes to intimidate and bully and lead with fear.

Becoming a Loving, Conscious Leader

We are living in a society that has embraced fear as a means to coerce others to do their bidding. In marketing, leadership, coaching, politics, education, health care, parenting, and religion, fear is the base operating system. In so many different ways, we have learned to rely on the stick and have forsaken the carrot. We have choices in how we act and how we encourage others. We can act because we are afraid not to do something, or because we love to do it—the choice between fear (separateness) and love (oneness).

The two words that spook people more than any others are the "S" and "L" words: *Soul*, and *Love*. Many people, including leaders, are afraid and embarrassed to include these words in their vocabulary because they have grown up with an internal message that plays as soon as they consider doing so: "If I express love or speak about the soul, people will think I am weak, flakey, or lacking in resolve, purpose, or strength."

> Human kindness has never weakened the stamina or softened the fiber of a free people. A nation does not have to be cruel to be tough.
>
> *Franklin D. Roosevelt*

But this kind of thinking is based on the erroneous belief that courage and strength are found in aggression (separateness) and that gentleness (oneness) reflects weakness. Leaders who believe that aggression is the best approach in any given situation, are, by definition, cowardly. As the Iroquois put it, "The greatest strength is gentleness."

There is a cultural impetus to our behavior, too. In his book *The Geography of Thought: How Westerners and Asians Think Differently and Why* (Free Press, 2004), Richard E. Nisbett notes that the Western mind is more focused on individuals and their distinctions—separation—while the Eastern mind is more focused on the (potentially harmonious) relationships between individuals—oneness. This may account for the growing interest in Eastern philosophy among leaders in the West.

Robert Stiller, CEO of Green Mountain Coffee Roasters, is among many leaders who have recognized the benefits of meditation. Employees at the Waterbury, Vermont, firm enjoy a soundproof space at company headquarters, where they are led in relaxation, visualization, and breathing exercises. Stiller has been meditating since the 1970s, and thought that his 400 employees might be more effective if they occasionally did absolutely nothing.

"Your best thoughts often come when you're in a relaxed state, like in the shower," Stiller says. "Meditation provides the space for that to happen."

Employees report that they have more energy and focus—and presumably are able to blend Eastern and Western approaches with a cup of java where necessary!

The Power of Love to Dispel Ego and Judgment

> What's encouraging about meditation is that even if we shut down, we can no longer shut down in ignorance. We see very clearly that we're closing off. That in itself begins to illuminate the darkness of ignorance.
>
> *Pema Chodron*

Paula Rosario is a marketing executive with an international research and promotion company in New York City. A servant-leader at heart, she developed an interest in coaching and applied her coaching skills and passion for inspiring others with several of her staff members, focusing on such issues as communication, leadership, and self-management. She soon discovered how the ego can get in the way of heart-to-heart communication when we allow ourselves to be swayed by personal judgments of others—in other words, when we do not love them.

Paula found one of her staff members to be particularly challenging to work with because of the perceived level of ego she encountered. Paula didn't approve of her values and opinions, and she was disappointed at being unable to feel genuine fondness towards her. But she knew that she could not be an effective leader and coach unless she could successfully look beyond the personality and communicate with this person at a deeper level.

> Everything that irritates us about others can lead us to an understanding of ourselves.
>
> *Carl Jung*

Paula decided that, during the next coaching session, she would turn down the sounds of her ego-mind and try to connect with her new colleague at the heart level.

If you judge people,
you have no time
to love them.

Mother Teresa

"I knew that, deep inside, people are more the same than they are different," says Paula, "and I made a conscious effort to find this place of oneness in our relationship."

That is when a transformation occurred. The invisible tension between the two of them seemed to evaporate, only to return temporarily whenever Paula's thinking was turned toward judgment, rather than understanding and compassion. It was a dance—whenever Paula moved forward with judgment, the new team member moved back; when Paula approached her with openness, she moved forward.

From this, Paula realized that she needed to put aside her preconceived ideas of her colleague and interact from a place of loving non-judgment. She had to walk in the other person's shoes.

"As I did this," remembers Paula, "my compassion for her grew immensely, and I was able to offer suggestions for alternative behavior and actions in a compassionate way."

Paula also decided to include the new team member in plans for the department. As she shared her thoughts and visions on projects with her, the doors of creative communication began to open, and the individual became more receptive to Paula and to the thoughts and opinions of others. Possibilities became realities. The enhanced communication began to build trust, and trust began to build respect.

Soon, the new team member became more positive in her expressions and openly shared with Paula how she was making progress in her personal life as well.

As Paula observed the individual becoming more involved and committed in her work, she herself experienced a profound healing that she carries with her to this day. It is a reminder to her that when we relate with others in a loving way, from the heart, it helps us to recognize oneness over separateness and put aside all external differences—they simply become irrelevant—and our hearts can open.

We can all learn from Paula's experience. We don't have to like someone to love them, but as conscious leaders, we must strive to see the sacredness in others—that which inspires us to look beyond the personality and ego—beyond the warrior or bully-leader archetype, and into the soul of the other person. When we do this, our natural objective is to increase their well-being. We want to help and serve them in every way we can.

> After the verb "to love," the verb "to help" is the most beautiful verb in the world.
>
> *Bertha von Suttner*

Multitasking and the Decline of Brilliance

Notwithstanding all its benefits described earlier, technology can also become a veil that separates us from intimacy, causing us to be enthralled with the technology itself, rather than the most valuable purpose of the technology—the creation of oneness. The preoccupation with technology can cause us to forget to honor others—in other words, to show our love for them—by being truly present with them. If we make a Faustian bargain with technology, causing our lives to be cluttered with superficial demands, we will squeeze the slow time out of our days and lose the chance to listen to our souls and the souls of others. We will lose the precious opportunity to be lovingly present with them.

> You cannot truly listen to anyone and do anything else at the same time.
>
> *M. Scott Peck*

When we become overly invested in solving the small, the mundane, and the to-do-list-sized problems of life, we miss the chance to be one with others, to ask the truly important questions that lead to intimacy. In the process, we find ourselves dragging our weary minds to work or school or to our parenting roles, while leaving our hearts behind. We're exhausted, with no spark left for the deeper essence of life, and this is an empty, dark place from which to share our love for each other and the world and engage in intimate relationships—the greatest yearning of the soul.

If we truly wish to move from being tired to inspired, it will take courage, energy, creativity, and deep resources. The much-vaunted practice of multitasking, for example, impairs inspiration and leads to mediocrity. Experience someone talking to you and answering their e-mail at the same time, and you will understand what I mean. Doing lots of things at once leads to doing many things poorly. Multitasking may contribute significantly to the decline of inspiration and our ability to love others, because it creates separateness and thwarts depth, excellence, and intimacy. We might as well download our e-mail while we listen to a concert (which I have witnessed), or while we make love (which I have not!).

Prevalent in many organizations is what some are calling "overburdening": giving people more work than they can possibly do, while mistakenly believing that subjecting them to this additional pressure is going to bring out the best in them. This creates pressure-cooker conditions that may inevitably lead to more multitasking (so much to do, so little time) and therefore inferior work and a lack of personal meaning and fulfillment.

> If you observe a really happy man, you will find him building a boat, writing a symphony, educating his child, growing double dahlias or looking for dinosaur eggs in the Gobi Desert. He will not be searching for happiness as if it were a collar button that had rolled under the radiator, striving for it as a goal in itself. He will have become aware that he is happy in the course of living life twenty-four crowded hours of each day.
>
> *W. Beran Wolfe*

Mastery is an expression of the love and passion we have for an activity—the degree to which we are one with it. If we want to achieve mastery in anything—and therefore be inspired by our contribution—we need to direct our full, loving presence to one thing at a time, and accomplish it brilliantly, rather than do many things adequately. With people, this happens best when we focus our resources and talents by slowing down, empathizing, and serving others—by giving that rare gift: our full, loving attention.

The beautiful thing about inspiration is that it can naturally flourish in almost every aspect of our world, including organizational leadership, government, education, religion, media, healthcare, and communications, as well as the soul spaces that make up our everyday lives. This is because inspiration comes from that sacred center that is within us all: the loving spirit. We all yearn to love, not only those we are with, but also what we do.

The Courage to Love

It takes courage, strength, and commitment to build and sustain relationships that are based on love and therefore inspiration. Gandhi said, "Love is the prerogative of the brave." It takes courage to tell your colleagues how much you love their work, how much you love being part of a particular team or organization. And yet, those are the things that inspire people. We need love in every aspect of our lives, not just in our personal lives, but at work, too. We are whole beings. We are humans, not workers or functions who leave our need to be loved at home and then go to work—we are one.

Fear is the psychological, emotional, and spiritual opposite of love. No one is inspired by fear. People may be motivated by fear, but they are never inspired by it. *Everything* that inspires us comes from love, without exception. In fact, there is nothing in our lives from which we get inspiration that does not also give us love. If a sunset inspires you, it is because you love sunsets, feeling a sense of oneness with the myth, mystery, and magic of the sunset. If a person inspires you, it is because you love that person, feeling a sense of oneness with them. Love is the place that gives rise to inspiration.

Some time ago, we were celebrating the two-year anniversary of working closely with a very large company. During the ceremony, which was attended by hundreds of people, I was joined on stage by the company's CEO. As a symbolic gesture to signal that I was bringing to a close my long-standing involvement with them—that they were now ready to continue this work on their own and that our work had become their work and they would no longer rely on our guidance—I was about to hand him a large, burning candle, a passing of the torch, as it were. And as I approached the CEO, whom I had come to know very well during the time of our close work together, I said to him, "Joe, I love you."

> To love and be
> loved is to feel
> the sun from
> both sides.
> *David Viscott*

As I spoke those words, one could hear some in the audience suck in their breath—a few from the shock of hearing such a statement uttered in public, others from the innocence of the moment.

Here was an unusual occurrence in our culture: two men standing on a stage, saying that they loved each other and truly meaning it. And very few felt that this was a weird thing to do; unusual, yes, but there was nothing odd about it. If we truly want to inspire people, then we should communicate the love that we feel for them.

This CEO knew that I loved him. I didn't really need to say so. But I believe it strengthened him to hear it from me and to know that we have this sacred relationship with each other, and it definitely strengthened me greatly. He has moved to another CEO position now, at a company three times larger, but we continue to be close friends—and we love each other and have the courage to say so. Love inspires all who are connected to it.

Sometimes, it helps to look at any given situation and learn to ask:

- What do I love about this situation?
- How can I be more loving in this situation?
- What would a person with a loving heart do right now?

The Power of a Loving Gesture

In fact, love can be expressed in even the most common interactions. Imagine that you are seated in a restaurant, and your waiter approaches you with this greeting: "The purpose of this restaurant is to inspire you. We want you to leave more inspired and loved than you were when you arrived. Please complete this card indicating your current level of inspiration—our aim is to do everything we can to increase your personal score by two points. How can I make this evening's dining experience an inspiring occasion for you?"

What a profound shift you might experience in your mood, your thoughts, and your spirit—and the gratuity might grow, too! Imagine what we could accomplish if we repeated this approach in each of our workplaces, churches, schools, hospitals, or homes. Approaching others with a loving heart is perhaps the single most powerful action we can take to build inspiring relationships, between politicians and their constituents, teachers and students, suppliers and customers, priests and parishioners, leaders and followers, coaches and clients, husbands and wives, or parents and children.

Love Inspires: A Tale from the Air

Scott Simmie, a reporter with the *Toronto Star* newspaper, was on Air Canada flight 792 from Los Angeles to Toronto, when he observed flight attendants passing down the aisle, briefly opening every overhead bin and peering inside. Something seemed unusual. It wasn't until a few minutes later, when the public address system came on, that Scott learned what was going on. The flight attendant who had earlier been dispensing drinks made a personal appeal to passengers, informing them that the change purses containing the money she had collected for the drinks had gone missing.

"If passengers would please take a look around their seats, I'd really appreciate it," she said. "I'm a single mother and I'm responsible for that money."

Passengers stopped watching the movie and began searching on the floor and looking around their seats for the stray purses. When nothing turned up, a young couple seated in row 16 felt inspired to take action: They decided to start a collection among passengers to make up the missing funds, which amounted to approximately $200.

"Please, don't," the flight attendant said, on the verge of tears. "That's so nice of you, but I just couldn't—you shouldn't—."

But the couple in row 16 ignored her pleas.

"Hey, people," they shouted throughout the craft, "The flight attendant hasn't found that money, and we'd like to take up a collection. If you can contribute anything, that would be great."

The other passengers didn't take long to respond, sending bills of five, ten, and even twenty dollars down the aisles to the friendly folks that had started the collection, who, shortly after, presented the flight attendant with a thick wad of bills.

"If there's anything extra, just give it to your favorite charity," they told her.

On the verge of tears and feeling overwhelmed with gratitude for the kindness just extended to her, the flight attendant picked up the mike to thank the passengers.

"I'm a bit close to tears at this point," she said, the emotion catching her throat. "I cannot express my gratitude for your kindness. I wish I could send each and every one of you a simple thank-you. It's an amazing thing to see so much spirit among so many of you. I'm totally overwhelmed by the whole thing."

She paused for a moment and then concluded with, "My best wishes to all of you, always."

An ordinary flight, with an extraordinary lesson that touched the hearts of many, including that of the pilot, who applauded the passengers' remarkable spontaneous act of kindness. It had made this flight unforgettable for all, and likely offered a profound lesson even for the individual who had taken the money. No one knows what happened to the stolen funds, but perhaps the enormous outpouring of goodwill from everyone aboard softened the culprit's heart. As Scott Simmie later wrote, this flight "brought out the worst in someone...and the best in others."

Love has an infinite and cascading capacity to inspire, as reflected in the loving initiative of the young couple in row 16 who were moved to help a single mother who stood to lose $200 of her personal money. Although the flight attendant was a stranger to them, they connected heart-to-heart, not only with her, but also with the other passengers on the flight. It was love and compassion—a sense of oneness—that inspired them to take the initiative to ask others to contribute, and love inspired the overwhelming response of kindness and generosity from other passengers. It inspired Scott Simmie, who wrote the story in an article for the *Toronto Star*, so that thousands of readers could also be inspired. It inspired people to post the story on blogs and bulletin boards read by flight crews on the Internet. On the day the article was posted on the *Star*'s Web site, it was the single most e-mailed news story that day. And if you and others who read this book feel inspired by this story, the wave of inspiration born on that journey through the skies has yet to reach the farthest corner of the Earth.[13]

Keeping It Simple—Loving Each Other and Telling the Truth

Sometimes, we simply make things way too complicated. There has been much written recently that intends to guide our lives towards meaning, fulfillment, and inspiration. Centuries ago, the

---

13. On Flight 792, a miracle at 35,000 feet, *Toronto Star*, October 8, 2004

Bible, the Qur'an, the Buddhist Sutras, the Tao Te Ching, the Bhagavad Gita, the Torah, and the I Ching all told a similar story: we are one—*love others.*

Inspiration begins with the love of others—not the love of oneself. We've all heard the cliché "love yourself first" so many times. This seems so typical of our narcissistic era. It is difficult to imagine any great historic teacher saying, "First, I must love myself." Love is not about oneself or one's ego. Loving others does not depend on first loving ourselves. In fact, it is the opposite. We will see an increase in the love we feel for ourselves, and the love received from others, when we love and serve others more.

Many experts have sold us on the idea of loving ourselves first, and we've been in therapy with this idea for 30 years trying to learn it. But this may not be the most effective path to happiness, let alone enlightenment. *Love is not about you*—it is about the other person. Love is a verb—it is the spontaneous action from row 16, when two hearts fill with love for another and they act on it. I am not suggesting that we need to sacrifice all our own needs in our efforts to love and serve others—just that we will gain the meaning, self-esteem, and love we all crave by first giving it to others, who will, nearly always, be inspired to reciprocate. And if they don't— and, as I have mentioned earlier, 2 percent of the time this will be the case—we can be philosophical about it, simply accepting it as part of life, like the Zen Master who gave away his clothes, instead of running our lives on the basis of the exceptions.

Loving Others Is Not a Program— It's a Way of Life

We learn how to love others by *doing it.* Vancity is a remarkably successful business having created a unique category—a one-of-a-kind entity that is beyond a bank, and beyond a thrift (legally, it is a cooperative).

Vancity describes itself as having one hand in the soil and one hand on the stars—being rooted and reaching. It's a concept that unites Vancity's six-decade history (rooted) and their future (reaching) into a succinct statement of who they are: secure, grounded, and networked, as well as aspirational, visionary, and thriving.

The organization is owned by account holders and other clients and, for a bank, embraces a unique set of beliefs:

We believe in the essential goodness of people.
We believe that dreamers are as unique as their dreams.
We believe that to rise higher, you must dig deeper.
We believe that balance in all things is the true measure of prosperity.
Wherever you are,
Whatever it is,
We believe you can.

Vancity believes that when "who we are meets what we believe, things grow here," because that is the natural result of a rooted-and-reaching organization that believes all things to be possible. And it is Vancity's central purpose, across all Vancity's departments, branches, and levels, to grow things: people, ideas, hope, finances, neighborhoods, and the dreams of Vancity's members—all emanating from a philosophy of oneness.

Dreaming, reaching for the stars, the goodness of people—to some, this may seem hopelessly naïve. But take a look at the numbers: Vancity is Canada's largest credit union, with $10.5 billion in assets, more than 300,000 members, 2,000 employees, and 42 branches throughout Greater Vancouver, the Fraser Valley, and Victoria in British Columbia, Canada. In 2004, it donated $13.5 million to local community organizations and members—an unheard-of 30 percent of earnings. The country's eight largest banks, by comparison, donated just 1 percent of theirs.

Many companies talk about how important their people are, but fewer live these ideas. At Vancity, employees receive three weeks of vacation in the first year and the option to exchange unused benefits for additional vacation days, as well as low-interest loans, mortgages and credit lines, tuition subsidies, and transit subsidies for Vancouver's light rail transit system. The head office, which is above a train station, features meditation rooms and private areas for nursing mothers, an employee-run library, and subsidized parking for those who carpool. The company pays the full cost of a flexible benefits plan. Bonuses are calculated as a percentage of Vancity's profits. Twenty-seven-year-old Mike Harris, who greets and directs people as they enter the branch, earned a bonus of 16 percent of his salary, enough to cover half his down payment on a new house. In 2003, Vancity received more than 12,000 applications from people who wanted to work there, and in 2005, they were voted Canada's Best Place to Work by *Maclean's* magazine.

> I'd rather be a could-be if I cannot be an are;
>
> Because a could-be is a maybe who is reaching for a star.
>
> I'd rather be a has-been than a might-have-been. By far;
>
> For a might-have-been has never been, but a has was once an are.
>
> *Milton Berle*

The essential truth for us all is that we are happiest when we are loved. Many traditional leaders will roll their eyes, but people today are yearning for the opportunity to be loved and to love—*at work*. And the non-eye-rolling conscious leaders, like Vancity's CEO, Dave Mowat, are tapping into this reality and growing their businesses.

"Ultimately," Mowat says, "if you think 'happy people' is artsy-fartsy, touchy-feely stuff, you can draw a direct, straight-line relationship to the financial success of your company. It is just a fact that the higher the morale of your organization, the more money you make. When people are engaged, they create trust, because they are happy. And they provide better service because they are more interested."

Mowat is an unusual leader. He *loves* people. He listens to *hear*, and he listens to make sure people feel loved and heard. He listens so that he can take action on what he hears. Shortly after becoming CEO of Vancity, he initiated a process requiring all the senior executives in the company to visit all of the local branches and head office each quarter to listen in the same way he does. This is how he achieves a consistent culture at Vancity. He bends the rules to the needs of employees and praises failure when it is part of learning. He makes fun of himself, has no airs or pretensions, and is humble, vulnerable, and fearless. His love for people, his work, his family, and his community is worn openly and unapologetically. He views all of the parts and the people in his life as one—and loves them all.

Listen. Do not have an opinion while you listen because frankly, your opinion doesn't hold much water outside of Your Universe. Just listen. Listen until their brain has been twisted like a dripping towel and what they have to say is all over the floor.

Hugh Elliott,
Standing Room Only
weblog, 02-14-2003

The Downtown Eastside is one of the oldest neighborhoods in Vancouver, Canada, and the historic heart of the city. It is a community rich in history, architecture, and diverse groups of people. In recent years, it has struggled with many of the complex challenges facing other big-city neighborhoods, such as drug addiction and dealing, HIV infection, prostitution, crime, lack of adequate housing, high unemployment, and the loss of many legitimate businesses.

With the impending closure of Vancouver's Four Corners Community Savings in early 2004—which would have left as many as 3,000 residents with no access to core banking services—Mowat saw the opportunity to utilize Vancity's financial and technological infrastructure in a cost-effective way to provide those services through a unique hybrid organization. He felt a responsibility to practice Vancity's commitment to social justice and financial accessibility—viewing the whole community as one—by providing residents of Vancouver's notorious Downtown Eastside community continued access to the banking services they need. Many residents of this community, often referred to as the nation's "poorest postal code," are homeless, ill, or involved in lives of drug addiction, prostitution, and crime.

Vancity embarked on a new initiative with PHS Community Services Society (Portland Hotel Society), a long-standing not-for-profit organization in the neighborhood, to create Pigeon Park Savings. Vancity commissioned famed architect Arthur Erickson to design the facility. When Pigeon Park Savings opened, the normal ID requirements were waived and new processes developed that were more in line with the needs of people who lived on the streets. The result was a self-sustaining enterprise offering core banking services (check-cashing, deposits and withdrawals, and debit cards) in a supportive and non-threatening environment at a minimum cost to Downtown Eastside residents, particularly those who face barriers in using a traditional financial institution.

All of the infrastructure, including IT and ATM support, administration services, training, and ongoing security and fraud support, is provided by Vancity, while Pigeon Park Savings is operated by skilled staff members who have extensive street experience working with members of the Downtown Eastside community.

Sharing the natural loving nature within us all is encouraged at Vancity.

Another project, the Potluck Café Society, grew out of a youth-at-risk employment initiative in 2000. Its initial funding was provided by the Vancity Community Foundation and the Vancity Community Solutions Fund. Today, it operates a café on the main level of the Portland Hotel, an acclaimed housing project in Downtown Eastside. Potluck provides full-time training employment for ten formerly-at-risk residents of the neighborhood. The Potluck Café Society does not expect everyone to make quick transitions, so they are committed to employing staff until they are ready to move on. The café also provides nutritious meals to area residents and a discounted daily breakfast, lunch, and dinner for low-income diners.

The Potluck Café Society is a social enterprise, relying on catering revenues and limited fundraising to help subsidize their programs, which in turn helps them to grow the number of meals served to area residents, ensure that the café is financially self-sustaining, and create additional sustainable jobs. Its purpose is to help transform the lives of individuals in this community.

Traditional banks charge more than the disadvantaged can afford each time they have their checks cashed. These people need to find work and to reintegrate themselves into society, but traditional banks see them as separate, low-profit-generating consumers. Mowat and Vancity see them as one—as people who need a place *where my heart touches your heart and adds to who we both are as persons.*

Conscious leaders are not afraid to be loving leaders, relating with their communities, customers, employees, suppliers, and others in a *loving*—not competitive or aggressive—way. What may seem unconventional or "artsy-fartsy," as Dave Mowat puts it, is, in reality, the hardheaded wisdom behind a great organization.

Practicing Oneness by Reclaiming Our Capacity to Love and Be Loved

When we discuss the word "love" in our organizations, some people's eyes roll, and some think that love is an emotion and a feeling that has no place in the work environment. But we are *whole* human beings, our lives are not separate, disconnected pieces—we are one—and we yearn to be loved and to love in every part of our *whole* lives, whether at work or at home. Many leaders limit their greatness by failing to resolve their emotional insecurities, thus remaining unable to show or share their emotions. Here are some thoughts to help clear the debris from our path to oneness:

- What prevents us from being able to freely express our love for others?
- What steps are we taking to remove old wounds and beliefs that will allow us to love freely?
- Are we telling those whom we love how we feel, or is it a secret that they have not yet heard from us directly?
- When we hear from someone that they love us, we are inspired and our hearts are filled. Who needs to be inspired this way— to experience these same feelings by hearing them from your heart?
- The greatest leaders are the most loved. Love is your key to greatness. Are you a leader who is loving and loved?
- With whom will you practice in order to learn and perfect the habit of loving fully?
- Who needs you to love them—now?

BOTTOM LINE

Why do we need to be Loving?
Because the greatest human need is to Love and
be Loved—in every part of our lives—at work
and in our personal lives. It is what builds great
relationships—everywhere. We are one.

REFLECTIONS TO INSPIRE GROWTH IN LOVE

In your life so far, when was your finest moment of offering unconditional Love to others? Describe this example of when you were at your personal, most Loving best:

_____

_____

_____

_____

_____

_____

Describe a current situation in your life that, in your heart, you know would be enhanced if you were to be more Loving. It is within you already, so how would you practice the same level of unconditional Love, from your own experience described above, in this current situation?

_____

_____

_____

_____

_____

_____

To love is to receive a glimpse of heaven.
Karen Sunde

10

EFFECTIVENESS

AMELIE NOISEUX LEARNED early in life that being truthful brings sweeter rewards to the soul than praise and prizes earned deceitfully. Like many nine-year-old school girls, she was anxious to please her teacher. One day, a perfect opportunity to do so presented itself. Just before lunch, the teacher asked the class a question, promising a sticker as a reward for the student who answered it correctly. Amelie didn't know the answer. She was relieved when the bell rang and the teacher said the discussion would continue after lunch.

Amelie ran out into the schoolyard and quickly found her sister, who attended a higher grade in the same school. Amelie's sister was able to tell her the answer to the teacher's question.

After lunch, Amelie was the first to raise her hand and answer the question, which the teacher acknowledged as correct. But while she was anticipating her promised reward, she heard the strong voice of conscience. Pride and satisfaction were suddenly replaced with feelings of shame and embarrassment.

"I knew the answer," Amelie heard herself saying to teacher and class, "but it didn't come from me—I asked my older sister."

> There is more in us than we know. If we can be made to see it, perhaps, for the rest of our lives we will be unwilling to settle for less.
>
> *Kurt Hahn, Founder of Outward Bound*

To her surprise, the teacher replied: "I overheard you speaking to your sister during lunch, and I was wondering if you would tell us the truth. I am so proud of you because you were honest. You deserve two stickers as a reward."

Effectiveness is the result of commitment to the other CASTLE Principles. Amelie felt relieved and happy that she had found the courage to tell the truth. Telling the truth proved to be highly effective for Amelie—she earned two stickers—while not being truthful would have secured her only one. She earned the love of the teacher and the respect of her classmates. And she learned a lesson about truthfulness that has guided her life since.

Twenty years later, I received a phone call.

"Dr. Secretan?"

"Yes," I replied.

"My name is Amelie Noiseux. The other day, you left a book on the airplane. I was in charge of the crew on your flight. I researched who was sitting in that seat, and I believe it was you. If it is your book, would you like me to send it to you?"

This is the stuff of which effective people are made. Conscious leaders who gather and inspire effective people like Amelie build great organizations around them. That is because such people understand, from a sense of oneness, that I am an integrated part of your world, that when I serve you, I serve myself, and that, as one, we make things work more effectively—personally and professionally.

Perspective: Lessons from an Artist

My friend Don Campbell, who is vice-president of product innovation and technology at software giant Cognos Incorporated, described this wonderful example of perspective and oneness:

My most recent experience with oneness comes from a new hobby. For years, I'd wished I could draw. Unfortunately, even my "stick men" were so poorly constructed that it was hard to identify them as such. I marveled at those who had the talent to draw, when obviously, I had none. Despite the apparent hopelessness of the task, I scoured the Internet for information and checked out a backbreaking amount of books from our local library.

After pouring through both theory and practice, I took those first bold steps into an area that I felt was sure to give me grief and be littered with disappointment. I bought the necessary beginner's supplies and started working through the exercises. I turned out to be as bad at drawing as I had feared. Luckily, this was both explainable and surmountable. It seemed that I had been looking at my subjects the wrong way—through the lens of separateness. To me, a face was made up of eyes, a nose, lips, ears, hair, and a few other details. My brain knew how to quickly substitute a known representation for these elements and plop them onto the page. It made drawing quick, but far from accurate.

You see, every face is different. Every expression is unique. From light and shadow to shape and contour, I wasn't representing what I saw, but rather what I thought I saw. When I realized that every part of the face blended seamlessly into every other part, that the beauty and subtlety of the face were in how it all worked together, I was able to look at that face differently—as one—and draw it appropriately. There had never been anything wrong with my fingers or hands, or how they had moved to make lines on the paper. The problem had been with my eyes and my brain and how I interpreted what I saw.

After only a few short months of working with my new hobby, I am amazed at what I can now produce! While practicing my drawing skills on a recent plane ride, some of the flight attendants referred to me as an artist. In truth, I'm just an infant learning to see. And I can't look at a face now without seeing the flow of its skin and the way the light dances, reflects, and hides along its many curves. What a beautiful sight!

As Don Campbell shows us, the practice of seeing life in separate pieces can sometimes block our path to effectiveness and fulfillment. Often, we make a breakthrough when we see the whole—the oneness of what we are observing.

Perspective: Lessons Learned in Space

In some ways, how effective we are depends on our perspective.

Buzz Aldrin, the lunar-module pilot of *Apollo 11*, once discussed oneness and his view of the Earth from the moon:

The soft, glowing presence of planet Earth in the black abyss had a pristine clarity uncaptured by photographs," he said. "Images on film lack the subtle shades, the brightness, and the depth of the living sphere, which bulged out of the blackness as I sailed outward on APOLLO 11... *From the deep blue of the Mediterranean, all of Europe and Africa sprawled away in soft pastels, innocent of political boundaries. And from the surface of the moon, where I could cover with my thumb the site of all human history, the Earth seemed fragile as a Christmas ornament, drifting like a lost balloon on the black velvet of space. The image of a living Earth, capable of extinction, disarms illusions of individual or tribal isolation. We gained more than altitude in those 66 years from* KITTY HAWK *to the moon. Seeing Earth not as an extension of man, but man as an extension of Earth.*

Gene Cernan, commander of *Apollo 17*, offered this perspective: "It was something so awe-inspiring you had to sneak a glance at it every chance you got. It's too beautiful to have happened by accident. To me, it was like sitting on God's back porch, looking back home."

> When people thought the Earth was flat, they were wrong. When people thought the Earth was spherical, they were wrong. But if you think that thinking the Earth is spherical is just as wrong as thinking the Earth is flat, then your view is wronger than both of them put together.
>
> *Isaac Asimov*

It's a matter of perspective, isn't it? As Marcus Aurelius said, "Everything we hear is an opinion, not a fact. Everything we see is a perspective, not the truth." How we see things depends on our viewpoint. We might observe that Buzz Aldrin and Gene Cernan were incredibly courageous—I feel queasy when I imagine myself sitting, as they did, thousands of miles out in space, looking back at my family, heritage, civilization, species, and potential legacy. Yet their courage was greatly rewarded. For Aldrin and Cernan—and for Amelie Noiseux—courage, authenticity, service, truthfulness, and love produced incredible rewards. That's what we call effectiveness.

Earlier, we discussed the shortcomings of a data-only perspective, but data is *one* of the necessary components of effectiveness, because metrics enable us to measure our effectiveness. Buzz Aldrin and Gene Cernan could never have conveyed the beauty of their experience with data alone. There is a paradox at work here: as in any great project, many data were necessary to put them in the position from which they described their experiences, *and*, before those data and metrics could be achieved, myth, mystery, and magic were required.

The Data Sandwich

True effectiveness begins with a dream—a vision drawn from myth, mystery, and magic. Realizing the dream then rests on the gritty details of mastery for effective implementation—engaging data and metrics to achieve the dream. After we successfully realize the dream, we celebrate the creation of new myths, mysteries, and magic. All dreams are realized that way—that's how we put a man on the moon.

Think of it as a data sandwich, with two outer layers of myth, mystery, and magic—one for dreaming the dream and another for realizing the dream. Between these, imagine a layer of mastery—data, as well as metrics, implementation, and execution—drawing deeply from the intellect and reason. The outer and inner layers combined represent the marriage of science and myth, mystery, and magic.

In a speech to Congress on May 25, 1961, President John F. Kennedy invoked the imagination of the world with these words: "I believe that this nation should commit itself to achieving the goal before this decade is out, of landing a man on the moon and returning him safely to the Earth." They were words of pure myth, mystery, and magic—the vision, the first layer of the sandwich.

> I'm an idealist without illusions.
> *John F. Kennedy*

Eighteen months later, at Rice University in Houston, Texas, Kennedy reaffirmed America's commitment to landing a man on the moon before the end of the 1960s. He spoke in philosophical terms about the magic of solving the mysteries of space:

No man can fully grasp how far and how fast we have come, but condense, if you will, the 50,000 years of man's recorded history in a time span of but a half-century. Stated in these terms, we know very little about the first 40 years, except at the end of them, advanced man had learned to use the skins of animals to cover them. Then about ten years ago, under this standard, man emerged from his caves to construct other kinds of shelter. Only five years ago man learned to write and use a cart with wheels. Christianity began less than two years ago. The printing press came this year, and then less than two months ago, during this whole 50-year span of human history, the steam engine provided a new source of power. Newton explored the meaning of gravity. Last month elec-

> America has tossed its cap over the wall of space.
> *John F. Kennedy*

tric lights and telephones and automobiles and airplanes became available. Only last week did we develop penicillin and television and nuclear power, and now if America's new spacecraft succeeds in reaching Venus, we will have literally reached the stars before midnight tonight.

Dreams that draw on the myths, mysteries, and magic of life will founder if the second layer—the science, mastery, implementation and execution, data, and metrics—are not included. It is these practical aspects that make the dream real. And so it was with Kennedy's space initiative. In the years that followed the Rice University speech, the intellect, mastery, and rational thinking of some of the greatest scientific minds in the world were engaged in manifesting this dream, though not without practical challenges. As Kennedy found, successful implementation requires that everyone engaged in the data and scientific stages of a project—the middle layer of the sandwich—is frequently reminded of, and inspired by, the original dream. Kennedy repeatedly held before the scientists the inspiration of myth, mystery, and magic, as the scientists experienced the scientific and technical challenges of making the dream real.

When Kennedy asked the NASA Administrator, James Webb, if he considered the moon-landing to be NASA's top priority, Webb replied, "No sir, I do not. I think it is *one* of the top priority programs."

This caused Kennedy to realize the risks involved in advancing the myth, mystery, and magic of his dream beyond the capacity of the science, mastery, data, and metrics to deliver it. He emphasized to Webb that it should be *the* top priority.

> Do you realize the responsibility I carry? I'm the only person standing between Richard Nixon and the White House.
>
> *John F. Kennedy*

"This is important for political reasons, international political reasons," he said, as he underscored the dream. "We ought to get it really clear that the policy ought to be that this is the top priority program of the agency and one...of the top priorities of the United States government. Otherwise we shouldn't be spending this kind of money, because I am not that interested in space. We've wrecked our budget and all these other domestic programs, and the only justification for it, in my opinion, is to do it in the time element I am asking."

This statement, gleaned from new research from the Kennedy Library, is remarkable. It shows that, contrary to our prior beliefs, Kennedy was not in love with the adventure into space so much as he was with America doing something bold, thus demonstrating world-class prowess in innovation and creativity. The launch of the *Sputnik* by Russia on October 4, 1957, had changed everything, catching the world's attention and the American public off-guard. In fact, the creation of NASA in July 1958 was one of America's reactions. Kennedy's real objective was to reverse America's sense of space envy and boost national self-esteem.

Kennedy offered a bigger dream than landing on the moon. For him, space was an opportunity to restore American myth, mystery, and magic— to create something so psychologically and emotionally compelling that it would inspire America and diffuse Russia's enmity. Historians often attribute the end of the Cold War to President Ronald Reagan and the Strategic Defense Initiative, dubbed "Star Wars," but Kennedy's psychological repositioning of the U.S. relative to Russia may have been much more instrumental. Kennedy connected Americans to the myth, mystery, and magic of space, and the seeds were thus sown for the eventual removal of the Iron Curtain.

> The quiet that envelops space makes the beauty even more powerful. And I only hope that the quiet can one day spread to my country.
>
> *Ilan Ramon, Israel's first astronaut, who died on the shuttle "Columbia"*

Kennedy had a gift for being just as inspirational with the data "filling" of the sandwich as he was with the outer layers of myth, mystery, and magic. This is conveyed in his speech at Rice University, where he focused on data to inspire people to follow his dream:

To be sure, all this costs us all a good deal of money. This year's space budget is three times what it was in January 1961, and it is greater than the space budget of the previous eight years combined. That budget now stands at $5,400 million a year—a staggering sum, though somewhat less than we pay for cigarettes and cigars every year. Space expenditures will soon rise some more, from 40 cents per person per week to more than 50 cents a week for every man, woman and child in the United States, for we have given this program a high national priority—even though I realize that this is in some measure an act of faith and vision, for we do not now know what benefits await us. But if I were to say, my fellow citizens, that we shall send to the moon, 240,000 miles away from the control station in Houston, a giant rocket more than 300 feet tall, the length of this football field, made of new metal alloys, some of which have not yet been invented, capable of standing heat and stresses several times more than have ever been experienced, fitted together with a precision better than the finest watch, carrying all the equipment needed for propulsion, guidance, control, communications, food and survival, on an untried mission, to an unknown celestial body, and then return it safely to earth, re-entering the atmosphere at speeds of over 25,000 miles per hour, causing heat about half that of the temperature of the sun—almost as hot as it is here today—and do all this, and do it right, and do it first before this decade is out—then we must be bold.

Kennedy was a master at weaving myth, mystery, and magic with the science, data, metrics, and all of the practical steps that are essential for the successful realization of a dream.

On July 21, 1969, Neil Armstrong became the first person to land on the moon, stepping onto its surface, in the Sea of Tranquility, at 0256 GMT, nearly 20 minutes after first opening the hatch on the *Eagle* landing craft. Buzz Aldrin remained in the lunar module and spoke the first words of man from the moon: "Tranquility base; the *Eagle* has landed." He followed

Armstrong to the surface 20 minutes later.

As Armstrong put his left foot on lunar soil, he famously declared, "That's one small step for man, one giant leap for mankind."

Meanwhile, Michael Collins informed mission control in Houston that he had successfully completed one orbit of the moon in the mother ship *Columbia* and the return trip was on schedule for 1750 GMT that evening.

The dream had been successfully realized. The world was starstruck by the myth, mystery, and magic of this dream to explore space. Ironically, or perhaps appropriately, for a man who said, "A man may die, nations may rise and fall, but an idea lives on," the President who conceived the dream did not live to see it realized. But his soaring vision inspired the world. Today, many Americans, and others, look back on this era as a golden age.

What makes a sandwich taste good is the combination of what is outside and what is inside. On their own, any one of data, mastery, implementation, myth, mystery, or magic lack flavor. It's the combination that's delicious and therefore effective.

> I think this is the most extraordinary collection of talent, of human knowledge, that has ever been gathered at the White House— with the possible exception of when Thomas Jefferson dined alone.
> *John F. Kennedy*

Effective Humans Are Inspired Humans

Our role as leaders is to inspire each other so that we locate and nourish the undiscovered greatness within us all. Effective humans always seek—and tend to find—each other. This is one of the attributes of great organizations. And communities of effective humans create greatness anywhere—in the race into space, at school, in corporations, at home, in church, in the world.

> Always do right— this will gratify some and astonish the rest.
> *Mark Twain*

These are not mutually exclusive ideas. Indeed, the reason why conscious leaders are effective is *because* they treat others as sacred and seek oneness by inspiring them *all the time*.

People-First Thinking = Ka-ching

But how will we measure effectiveness? Clearly the heroism of the warrior-archetype leader is no longer the best, or even the most relevant, benchmark with which to measure the effectiveness of leaders. Nor do the metrics of revenues, profit, margin, market share, or shareholder value, so dry on their own, measure enough. Conscious leadership is about unlocking the potential of humans, and that means the whole human, and *all* humans, not some of them or just the financial parts of them. And it is about enhancing the local and global communities we inhabit and being gentle with nature. We live in a real world, a world that comprises the personality *and* the soul. We are increasingly aware that we must succeed—that is, be effective—on both counts. Why? Because they are both one.

In 1972, twenty-three-year-old George Zimmer walked into Foley's Department store in Houston to sell the buyer some boys' raincoats made by his father's apparel company. The buyer convinced George, as part of the transaction, to take back $10,000 of unsold inventory from his father's company. But the next year, George's generosity was dishonored when the buyer dropped his father's line altogether.

Devastated, George invested $7,000 to lease a store of his own, selling men's suits below Foley's prices. Today, George's store has grown into the publicly listed Men's Wearhouse, with 700 North American stores, $1.7 billion in sales and 10,400 full-time employees.

More than 30 years after this experience, George observes, "As business people, we have a unique opportunity to write the rules, and it is not as complicated as some MBAs would like us to believe. In fact, the most important rule in business or in life was written thousands of years ago: 'Do unto others as you would have others do unto you.'"

George attributes his success to a deep commitment to his colleagues.

"It's simple," he says, "we're not in the suit business; we're in the people business. Everybody else is in the suit business." He adds, "We discovered that the quality of trust we built with the people who came through our doors depended on how well we trusted those with whom we worked."

Some years ago, George amazed Wall Street during a regular call to analysts by declaring that Men's Wearhouse valued its stakeholder relations in the following order:

1. Employees
2. Customers
3. Vendors
4. Shareholders
5. Communities served by Men's Wearhouse

The stock declined 20 percent the following day. This didn't concern George, however. He knew that he had shaken out the speculators and that those who understood the long-term implications of what he was building would invest in Men's Wearhouse for the long haul. And he was right—the stock has never looked back.

One of the most successful services offered by Men's Wearhouse is the rental of tuxedos, which was launched in 1999 and now exceeds one million annual rentals. As part of this business venture, the company decided to construct an in-house facility in Houston, Texas, for dry-cleaning tuxedos between rentals.

Several years earlier, in the early 1990s, George had invited Rinaldo Brutoco to join the board of Men's Wearhouse. Rinaldo, a successful international business executive, consultant, founder of the World Business Academy, and ardent environmentalist, was accustomed to taking a long-term, holistic view of organizations and business activities. When presented with the challenge of how to dry-clean tuxedos between rentals, he began investigating the most effective and environmentally appropriate way.

Dry-cleaning today is a business notorious for using toxic chemicals, principally perchloroethylene, better known as "perc," a volatile organic solvent proven to be toxic to the environment and hazardous to the health of people, especially those who work in dry-cleaning establishments. It gives clothes their distinctive, and biologically harmful, "just dry-cleaned" smell. Despite the risks, perc is still the number one dry-cleaning chemical in the world because it is considered to be the least expensive solution—not counting the damage to humans and the environment.

But Rinaldo and George saw perc as anything but economical, because they view the subject not as a separate activity, but as part of the whole—a view based on oneness that includes employees, customers, suppliers, the community, and the natural environment.

"The general perception in the industry is that eliminating perc is too expensive," says Rinaldo, "and it is a fact that using a non-toxic solvent is more capital-intensive and, therefore, initially more costly. But it also makes clothes last longer, and so can actually pay for itself."

It turns out that while perc may rid clothes of dirt, it does not do so gently; it is a harsh chemical that reduces a garment's life.

Financial managers were initially unimpressed with Rinaldo's proposals. They did not want to depart from industry-accepted standards, and they turned down his first suggestion to use carbon dioxide as a healthy and safe alternative to perc. Rinaldo presented an EPA-approved, silicon-based solvent as a second choice, but the financial managers dismissed this idea as well.

> A great many people will think they're thinking when they are merely rearranging their prejudices.
>
> *William James*

George reconfirmed his commitment to the people-centered values that are at the core of Men's Wearhouse, agreeing that he would simply not expose his employees to the hazards of perc in the Houston building. Based on this commitment, Zimmer invited Brutoco to provide an assessment—to create a data sandwich—which showed that the silicon-based solvent could extend the useful life of garments by 25 percent. This meant that tuxedos could be rented out for 25 percent longer before needing to be replaced. Brutoco argued that this financial benefit from the longer useful life of the garments would generate the additional revenue to pay for the increased costs of using the silicon-based solvent.

George's commitment to the health and well-being of people —inside his organization as well as in the community—would have led to the implementation of this people-friendly solution anyway, but Rinaldo's financial arguments proved to be the way to effectiveness—bringing everyone, including the financial team, on board, so that they could fully support the decision.

Today, Men's Wearhouse is the largest renter of tuxedos in North America, cleaning them all with non-standard, non-toxic materials that are harmless to employees, customers, and the environment, and even more effective than the toxic alternatives. The longer life of the suits increases the financial return on each one rented. In fact, Men's Wearhouse launched an independent cleaning company in Houston, using the EPA-approved silicon-based solvent, and in its first year, this business captured 21 percent of the city's entire dry-cleaning market.

George Zimmer's commitment to people through oneness and servant-leadership has helped to guide his company's continuous growth, and no end is in sight. He forecasts $3 billion in sales by 2010. This is especially remarkable considering that the U.S. tailored men's clothing market loses 2 to 3 percent in volume each year, the number of men's suits sold annually has dropped 40 percent to around ten million since 1994, and retail employees are among the lowest paid wage-earners, resulting in high staff turnover.

Effectiveness is the direct result of living the CASTLE Principles—being courageous, authentic, serving, truthful, and loving.

You might have noticed that almost all of the notable corporate examples cited in this book, including Men's Wearhouse, Wegmans, Starbucks, Southwest Airlines, and Alaska Wildland Adventures, and other great companies such as FedEx, Medtronics, and Pella, place people at the top of their priority list—ahead of customers or shareholders.

The application of the CASTLE Principles enables us to be optimally effective in all areas of life—at home, at work, at school, or wherever we are in relationships with others. Transformation is personal—it begins with the individual, as George Zimmer and Rinaldo Brutoco show us, but its effects spill over into our activities in extended environments and thus facilitate the transformation of others. Dishonoring 23-year-old George Zimmer may have appeared to be an isolated, separate incident to the Foley's buyer, but there are no actions without consequences—we are one.

Effectiveness as Economic Permission

Effectiveness in personal and corporate settings could be defined in some respects as *economic permission*, which is expressed as the profit, or positive cash flow, that enables us to continue to do the things to which we aspire in this world—as individuals and as organizations. Simply stated, money is energy, and the amount of money-energy flowing in must equal the money-energy flowing out, and this is equally applicable to individuals and organizations. By this measure, a lack of economic permission indicates ineffectiveness and thereby a loss of the privilege to be courageous, authentic, serving, loving, and truthful—the rest of the CASTLE Principles. Why? Because all of us can be more effective when we are courageous, authentic, serving, truthful, and loving—as individuals or organizations—when we earn, and are supported by, the economic permission to do so.

The absence of economic permission proved to be the undoing of Arthur Andersen, discussed in chapter 6. There can be little doubt that Arthur Andersen would be thriving today if its leaders had, at the time, been more courageous, more authentic, of greater service to others rather than themselves, more truthful, and

> The depth of your mythology is the extent of your effectiveness.
> *John Maxwell*

more loving. And if they had been all of these, they would have been more effective—they would have survived. But the withdrawal of economic permission removed their opportunity to be courageous, authentic, serving, truthful, and loving—even if they had chosen this path. Any business (or a family, church, hospital, school, fire department, city hall, or country) that practices the CASTLE Principles will become more effective, which means more successful, viable, masterful, inspiring, and loved. Thus, when we are effective in this way, our work is affirmed. We are a more inspiring and inspired community. And we are therefore able to increase our investments and continue to grow.

Effectiveness and the Whitewater Rule

In 1997, Sue Ellen Cooper, from Fullerton, California, then 53, was walking down a street in Tucson, Arizona, when she was stopped in her tracks by a red hat in the window of a thrift shop.

"I didn't need it," she says. "I had nowhere to wear it. There was no good reason to buy it ... Before I knew it, that bright red fedora was perched on my head, dipping daringly below one eyebrow."

Some months later, inspired by that hat, she gave a similar red hat and a copy of a well-known poem to a friend for a birthday gift. The poem, entitled *Warning*, by the British poet Jenny Joseph advises "making up for the sobriety of my youth," and begins with these lines:

When I am an old woman I shall wear purple
With a red hat which doesn't go and doesn't suit me.

As time passed, Sue Ellen gave similar gifts to three other close friends. In 1998, Cooper and these four women wore their red hats with purple outfits to high tea—and the group began—there were enough red hats for a tea party.

The idea—women of a certain age being visible and having fun—caught on quickly, and chapters grew across America and then Canada and around the world. Today, the Red Hat Society is what Cooper calls a "disorganization" of 42,000 chapters and over one million registered members, from all walks of life, in all 50 U.S. States and 30 countries, wearing anything from red cowboy hats for picnics, red southern belle hats for tea, red woolly hats for snowy days, and red baseball caps for casual wear.

The Society's aim is social interaction and encouragement of fun, silliness, and creativity. There are no initiations, fundraising projects, rules, or bylaws. Instead, there's just the tendency toward "Red Hattitude"—a willingness to stand out, hang loose, laugh at yourself, and have fun. This attitude will help when you are drafted into a local chapter with a name like the *Red Hat Belles*, the *Rah Rah Sisters*, the *Royal Red Hat Hotties* (or the *Red Hat Hoosier Hotties* if you are in Indiana), *the Rowdy Red Hat Mamas*, and the *Red Hot Flashes*.

> The great lesson from the true mystics is that the sacred is in the ordinary, that it is to be found in one's daily life, in one's neighbors, friends, and family, in one's backyard...To be looking elsewhere for miracles is to me a sure sign of ignorance that everything is miraculous.
>
> Abraham Maslow

"Here at *Hatquarters* in Fullerton, we sign up between 50 and 100 new chapters from around the world each day," says Cooper. "The names that the individual chapters come up with are hilarious. All new chapters are sent little feathers, which serve as reminders of the permission to be playful and have fun."

Only society members over 50 wear purple and red. Society members under that magic age wear pink hats and lavender outfits until they "reduate" (turn 50).

Founders of chapters are called queen mothers instead of presidents, and the other members are free to choose creative titles for themselves, such as Duchess of Fine Bone China, or Baroness of Button-Collecting. Sue Ellen Cooper is known as the Exalted Queen Mother, and she worries that making the Red Hat Society "another place to work on a committee" will spoil the fun.

> While we have the gift of life, it seems to me the only tragedy is to allow part of us to die— whether it is our spirit, our creativity or our glorious uniqueness.
> *Gilda Radner*

"This is totally a play group," she says, where members can have recess from taking care of others. We also aim to change people's perception of older women—we want them to be seen as valued members of our society."

What antics do Red Hatters get up to when they meet? Whatever they want. Sabrina Contreras, vice-president of merchandising and product development for the Red Hat Society, says, "We're off our rockers, not in our rockers. To our women, red means go."

Some chapters meet for dinner or lunch in full red-hat regalia just to chat. Many favor feather boas and blinky-light finger rings. Some meet at a restaurant once a month to sing Broadway show tunes. Others plan outings to museums, the theatre, or other enjoyable events. In August 2004, Red Hatters swarmed Branson, Missouri, for a Red Hat Convention. Thousands of Red Hatters from across the Midwest tried to break a kazoo-playing record, had a biggest-hat contest, participated in a pajama breakfast, took in the entertainment, and shopped. And Red Hatters *shop*: "The natural nature of women is to nurture. However, we're giving each other permission to go to recess," says founder Cooper.

Now, this may all seem like a little frivolous fun—but tune in to the effectiveness of this enterprise: At the Red Hat Society's annual convention at the MGM Grand Hotel in Las Vegas—one of the largest hotels in the city—more than 5,000 Red Hatters showed up for the sold-out Red Hat Society Big Deal Convention. Red Hatter conventioneers forked out $400 each to shop at a temporary 33,000-square-foot Red Hat Society store filled with Red Hat products and merchandise from 30 licensed partners. There is an official travel provider (Carlson) and a co-branded MasterCard, official Red Hat Society sneakers made by Keds, and Duncan Hines red velvet cake mixes. The group officially licenses Red Hat Society products, which range from Christopher Radko glass ornaments to needlework from Candamar Designs—and, of course, the hats. Merchandise can be purchased online at *redhatsociety.com* or at numerous retail outlets. The society launched a $4.99 monthly magazine—*LifeStyle: The Official Publication of the Red Hat Society*—which quickly grew to 33,000 subscribers. Sue Ellen Cooper wrote her first book, *The Red Hat Society: Fun and Friendship After Fifty* (Warner Books, 2004), which has sold around 500,000 copies, and followed it, in 2005, with *The Red Hat Society's Laugh Lines* (Warner Books).

Cooper works 40 hours a week supervising employees and serving Red Hatters in her Fullerton, California, office, answering questions, sending out Society materials, and registering new chapters. Cooper's husband, Allen, left a 32-year career in product development and sales to work full-time with the Society, taking care of technology and finances. Her daughter Andrea is vice-president of creativity.

The enormous success of *The Red Hat Society* reflects the great yearning for oneness that exists among women, including older women, who, just like other members of our society, want companionship, fun, and release from the seemingly endless number of responsibilities in life. The Society offers a platform for women from all over the world and many different backgrounds to come together in celebration of this spirit of oneness. "The universal acceptance of anyone who wants to become a member is very important to us," says Sue Ellen. "We want to make it easy for women to join."

It's the *Whitewater Rule*: Following the energy of passion and creativity, pursuing the principles of courage, authenticity, service, truthfulness, and love, leads to effectiveness.

"Are you familiar with the Toad ride at Disneyland?" Cooper asks. "That's what happened to my life. I was just going along and suddenly the track took this unexpected turn, all because of a red hat. It's been very exciting, and I am ready for whatever is next. I have been stretched immeasurably; I am more self-confident than I have ever been. Most importantly, the Red Hat Society is making a difference in women's lives, and that's of great value to me. The most important thing is that we grasp the importance of letting go and having fun, of giving ourselves permission to play. Once that happens, change has already begun, however subtle or grand it may be."

> It is not because things are difficult that we do not dare; it is because we do not dare that things are difficult.
>
> *Seneca*

An outrageous dream like flying to the moon, building a men's tailored clothing business in a way that is sensitive to people and the environment in a market that is declining, and inspiring women over 50 to have fun, contribute, and play—all are effective outcomes of living the principles of courage, authenticity, service, truthfulness, and love.

By tapping into our capacity to dream, reconnect with our myths, mysteries, and magic, and by following the simple notion that we are one, we are able to achieve remarkable things—even more remarkable than most people believed. We can inspire people and organizations, achieve national dreams, raise self-esteem, and achieve new standards of performance. Not through separation, but by knowing we are one.

Practicing Oneness by Reclaiming Our Effectiveness

What difference will it make to have lived your life? Are the dreams, intentions, and desires on which you have set your heart being attained? The point is to advance our lives towards the attainment of dreams and achievements for our organizations, our friends and families, ourselves, our communities, and our planet. Reflect on these thoughts to help you raise your personal and organizational effectiveness:

- What are you trying to achieve?
- Why?
- How will you measure this? How will you know that you have attained your dreams?
- Do you have the necessary courage to achieve your dreams?
- Are your dreams and intentions authentic?
- Who will be served by your achievements?
- Are your intentions honest and invested with truth?
- Do you love the aspirations you have set, and the reason for reaching them?
- Will they be attained in a loving way?
- How are you raising the capabilities necessary for you to realize your desired outcomes and dreams?
- Are you focused on results? Or are you focused on inspiring others, thus helping them to achieve results?
- Who is helping you? What is their investment in a successful outcome for you?
- Are you open to finding a "Red Hat"—that you don't need—following the energy, the *Whitewater Rule,* that might lead you to an even greater level of effectiveness than that for which you are now striving?

BOTTOM LINE

Why do we need to be Effective?
Because our lives, at work and at play, will be more successful and fulfilled when we achieve our physical, material, intellectual, emotional, and spiritual goals—when we are Effective.

REFLECTIONS TO INSPIRE GROWTH IN EFFECTIVENESS

What has been one of your most brilliantly Effective moments in life? Describe this example of when you were at your personal, most Effective best:

_____

_____

_____

_____

_____

_____

Describe a current situation in your life that, in your heart, you know would be enhanced through practicing greater Effectiveness. It is within you already, so how would you apply the same level of Effectiveness, described in your own experience above, to this current situation?

_____

_____

_____

_____

_____

_____

The secret of joy in work is contained in one word—excellence. To know how to do something well is to enjoy it.
Pearl Buck

CONCLUSION

The Evolution of Leadership

During the 1970s and 1980s, leadership practitioners and theorists alike began to recognize the inherent weaknesses in the command and control systems that had long dominated management thinking. The theory, literature, and practice of leadership began to take on a more human face by recognizing what we might call the "core people" (meaning customers and employees, in that order) at the heart of the organization and, therefore, a central focus of the attention of leaders. Customers and employees were no longer considered separate from the organization, but one with it.

This rising awareness existed uneasily as a partner with the established priorities of shareholders and other equity stakeholders. Note that only certain groups qualified as "core people," and notable exceptions remained outside this unit, including vendors, regulators, unions, competitors, media, politicians, environmentalists, and communities. These, along with the legacy for humanity, continued to be victims of separateness thinking. While these "other people" also attracted a certain level of attention, they were not important for their own sake. Instead, they were appreciated for their utility in being essential contributors or potential blocks to furthering the organization's strategic objectives. Therefore, this view represented a continuation of the philosophy of separateness, but with minor concessions to oneness.

During the late 1990s and early 2000s, a marked decline in people-centered thinking took place, sweeping the nascent focus on core people away with it. This reversion to the command-and-control style of leadership caused a regression that grew back, almost, to the levels attained in the 1970s. As the 2000s unfolded, however, the failures of the command-and-control, "extreme-capitalism" philosophy became clear—the long list of corporate failures, bankruptcies, criminal charges, environmental destruction, and plummeting employee and customer satisfaction ratings all told the same story: the command-and-control approach based on separateness was failing.

> When we try to pick out anything by itself, we find it hitched to everything else in the universe.
> *John Muir*

The response to this failure is the recent resurgence in conscious leadership founded upon a greater understanding of oneness. Treating employees, customers, vendors, and shareholders, for example, as being separate from the organization or the community or the world has been revealed to be a flawed idea—and many experienced the pain of working in such environments. As we are being reminded of this, we are beginning to understand and return to the essential truth of oneness again. And "return" is an important word here. As I have argued earlier in this book, oneness was the way we lived our lives thousands of years ago—the time of myth, mystery, and magic. But at that time, we were unconsciously practicing oneness—living it without understanding or valuing the sacredness of our oneness.

After sleeping through a hundred million centuries we have finally opened our eyes on a sumptuous planet, sparkling with color, bountiful with life. Within decades we must close our eyes again. Isn't it a noble, an enlightened way of spending our brief time in the sun, to work at understanding the universe and how we have come to wake up in it? This is how I answer when I am asked—as I am surprisingly often—why I bother to get up in the mornings.

Richard Dawkins

Now, we are being presented with a remarkable opportunity to become consciously aware of our oneness—this time with the understanding of how special and powerful oneness is. Practicing oneness without being aware of it is one thing; but living oneness and understanding why we are doing so is immeasurably more powerful. Being clear about the value of myth, mystery, and magic, and fully appreciating that we are all one, could enhance the quality, power, and opportunity for leadership and life in ways that we may never have broadly experienced before in human history.

When we choose to invoke the fear-based impulses of our ego, we invest negative energy in deepening the differences between us and others, thus strengthening our commitment to separateness. When we transcend this need by working more from our souls than our egos, we become aware of our inherent oneness and invest more time in living this way, thus making our oneness even stronger. Each day, we are presented with choices—separateness or oneness. It is up to us to choose wisely and change the world accordingly. With conscious awareness, we can see the same thing with different eyes.

On Having New Eyes

Marcel Proust wrote, "The real voyage of discovery comes not in seeking new landscapes, but in having new eyes." The CASTLE

Principles offer us new eyes—eyes with which to look around and marvel at our oneness and see the sacredness in others.

A surgeon who worked in a hospital of one of our health-care client firms told us that after learning the CASTLE Principles, he began to see both the patient and the scalpel through the lens of sacredness. He was already a top-flight surgeon, but now he viewed the scalpel as more than an instrument—he saw it as a *sacred* instrument. And he no longer viewed the patient as simply a "case"—but as a sacred being.

> I shall tell you a great secret, my friend: Do not wait for the last judgment; it takes place every day.
>
> *Albert Camus*

As a consequence, he performed his surgeries with even greater love and care. His patients told their friends of the extraordinary levels of skill and relationship he displayed, and, as a result, the hospital began to see a rise in new patients seeking treatment at his facility.

It didn't stop there. To the surgeon, the nurses and other attending clinical staff seemed now to look different also—sacred—and so he began treating them differently, too, from a courageous, authentic, serving, truthful, and loving place. With hospital nursing staff turnover typically hovering at 30 percent per annum, and 92 percent of nurses reporting they have experienced verbal abuse from physicians, this new attitude began to make a significant difference to the relationships among nurses, physicians, and other hospital staff. Instead of being upset, angry, and disinterested, they became inspired, and, over time, staff resignations declined.

The surgeon was thus inspired to have a nearly insatiable desire to view things anew. Looking through the lens of the CASTLE Principles, he began to see the sacredness in all of the equipment and facilities, respecting them in new ways. Respected equipment lasts longer, malfunctions less, and costs less to maintain and replace. Tensions, anger, and hostility subsided, and tolerance, understanding, and love grew.

As a result of all this, the entire operating room, and eventually the whole hospital, became transformed. Staff turnover declined, the depth of wisdom increased, mortality rates declined, clinical effectiveness increased, reputations grew, market share increased, and costs declined. The CASTLE Principles impacted every part of this organization and the lives of the people working there, as well as the lives of others who were part of the oneness of this health-care system—suppliers, patients, investors, regulators, and those served in the community.

This particular facility received top honors for the greatest reduction in heart attack mortality in a single year in an American hospital. Staff turnover dropped from 24 percent to 11 percent in nine months, resulting in annual savings of $70 million. Revenues increased, even though market conditions were depressed; profitability turned from near zero to one of the best in health care. This was the first health-care system in America to implement a Six Sigma initiative (a quality management program that aims to improve quality), but with a difference—they called it *Soulful Six Sigma* because, unlike many traditional Six Sigma programs, they guaranteed not to lay anyone off as a result of job eliminations following the implementation of Six Sigma processes.

Using the CASTLE Principles to see the oneness in all relationships is good for the bottom line and good for the soul.

The paradox is that, in all but one respect, everyone, and everything, has remained the same. The only difference is that employees in this organization are seeing the same things that they saw before, but this time with eyes that see the sacredness—the oneness—in others and in everything: a holiness of gaze.

That is the message of this book. The CASTLE Principles, when fully lived, enable us to see the sacred connections between everyone and everything—the oneness of people and things.

These six principles help us to reframe leadership and life. In our interchangeable roles as leaders and led, the daily practice of the CASTLE Principles of courage, authenticity, service, truthfulness, love, and effectiveness helps us to see the world with new eyes, revealing the sacred perspective of oneness and dissolving the illusion of separateness. This, then, becomes our new reality...

...the reality that we are...

 NE

Become a Member of the ONE Community

The last lines of John Lennon's ode to oneness, *Imagine*, invite us to community:

> *You may say I'm a dreamer,*
> *But I'm not the only one,*
> *I hope some day you'll join us,*
> *And the world will live as one.*

ONE is not just a book—it is one of the instruments in a growing movement to change the world by reawakening spirit and values in the workplace. If you would like to join this vibrant community of people who want to see more conscious leadership in the world, there are many avenues open to you.

How to Contact Us:

The Secretan Center Inc.
P.O. Box 1050
Erin, Ontario
N0B 1T0
Canada
Phone: 519-927-5213
Fax: 519-927-3909
E-mail: info@secretan.com
Web: http://www.secretan.com

Web Site:

Please visit our main Web site at http://www.secretan.com and the Web site for *ONE* at http://www.secretan.com/one. There, you will find many helpful ideas, a blog, free downloads, links to materials to support you in further study of *ONE*, and information on how to set up a *ONE* book discussion group.

Keynotes, Workshops, Retreats, Consulting, and Coaching:

To book Lance Secretan to address your conference, group, or organization, please go to this Web address:

http://www.secretan.com/meetingplanners.php

If you would like any of the Secretan Center faculty or coaches to work with you, please contact us through the above coordinates.

Learning More:

For resources you can use to bring *ONE* more fully into your life or your organization, please visit our Web site. There are teachers and coaches across the globe available to support you in your journey toward oneness.

http://www.secretan.com/one

INDEX